The Holy Spirit
— and —
the Gay Community

The Early Years

God's Love Reconciling the LGBTQ Community

REV. SAMUEL KADER

Most Scriptures quoted are from the HOLY BIBLE, NEW KING JAMES
VERSION [NKJV] Copyright ã 1982 by Thomas Nelson Inc.
Used by permission; all rights reserved.

Scripture is taken from the HOLY BIBLE, NEW INTERNATIONAL VERSION.
Copyright ã 1973, 1978, 1984 International Bible Society. Used by permission of
Zondervan Bible Publishers.

Other Scriptures used are otherwise noted.

Standard abbreviations used for other versions are as follows:

King James Version, [KJV]

New American Standard Version [NAS]

New King James Version [NKJV]

The Living Bible [TLB]

Table of Contents

The History of the Holy Spirit's Move Among Gays

In the beginning, God created the heaven and the earth. And the earth was without form, and void; and darkness was upon the face of the deep. And the Spirit of God moved upon the face of the waters. And God said, let there be light: and there was light.

And God saw the light, that it was good: and God divided the light from the darkness [1]. (Genesis 1:1-4)

This first chapter of the Bible could pretty much sum up how the movement of the Holy Spirit began among the gay, lesbian, bisexual, and transgender (LGBT) community. In the beginning, there was nothing but a spiritual void and darkness in that community. All the laws of the land criminalized same-sex love and relationships; all Christian churches condemned such love from the pulpit, and anyone who was gay or even suspected could never be a credentialed minister of the Gospel. Then the Holy Spirit began to hover over that darkness, and landed first in the United States, in a hospital room in Los Angeles.

Whenever God begins to do new work, He raises up a leader of that movement. There would be no exodus for the Jewish people were there not a Moses. God finds a person to change history: a Joan of Arc, a Martin Luther, a John Wesley, a William Wilberforce, a Martin Luther King Jr., and thus a movement begins.

Ever since October 6, 1968, with a gathering of twelve people in Rev. Troy Perry's living room in Huntington Park, California, the Holy Spirit has been moving among the gay, lesbian, bisexual, and transgender community, sweeping gay people and their friends into an unprecedented

1

move of God. What started as a primarily gay Christian church in one home in Los Angeles became a movement that far extended beyond the reaches of California, and beyond the scope of one denomination. It has been a sweeping worldwide revival.

Initially, Rev. Troy Perry held that first meeting in the living room of his home, but soon other ministers wanted to join him. Within a truly short time, the Metropolitan Community Churches were born and began popping up in every major metropolitan area of the United States, and even internationally in many other nations as diverse as Canada, Australia, and Nigeria.

This move of God has leaped across denominational lines, across theological lines and is still expanding. The Holy Spirit's scriptural mandate has focused on John 3:16, one of the most famous passages in the Gospels.

For God so loved the world that he gave his one and only Son, that whoever believes in him shall not perish but have eternal life.[2]

The focus is on the word: *whoever*. God loves the world and all those within it. Whoever chooses to come to Christ will not be cast aside. *Whoever* includes gay people. It does not take much effort to discover that within the Christian community there are many denominations and theological positions that refute that claim. They contend that it is impossible for gays, lesbians, bisexuals, and transgender people to come to Christ. If it were even possible, they contend, then they would have to deny their sexual orientation or gender identity. But they came too late to convince the millions of LGBT people and their supporters who know otherwise. When people have an encounter with God for themselves, an opposing theological viewpoint cannot convince them otherwise.

Jesus said in John 10:3-5, 27 that His sheep would know His voice, and that they would not listen to anyone else. God is still talking.

According to Elaine Sundby, the author of *Calling the Rainbow Nation Home*,[3] and the webmaster of www.Gaychurch.org currently there are now over 8,467 gay-friendly and affirming Christian churches that will fully embrace God's gay, lesbian, bisexual, and transgender children. This number keeps growing.

Bringing gay people into the Christian fold has been a journey fraught with dangers and pitfalls. Several challengers have tried to stop gay people from entering the Christian fold. Many of the churches within the LGBT Christian community have been defaced, threatened, or destroyed. Notably among them was the Metropolitan Community Church in New Orleans, Louisiana. The second-floor location where worship services were held was firebombed on Sunday, June 24, 1973. Thirty-two people died and numerous individuals were injured in that firebombing at the Upstairs Lounge at Iberville and Chartres Sts. It was reported to be the deadliest fire in New Orleans' history [4]. In 1973, only one New Orleans clergy, The Rev. William Richardson of St. George's Episcopal Church, was caring enough to hold an immediate service for the victims of this tragic event and their families. Then, a week later, St. Mark's United Methodist Church allowed Rev. Troy Perry to hold a memorial service for these members of Metropolitan Community Church.

Among those killed in the fire was the Pastor of the MCC, Rev. William R. Larson, Duane George "Mitch" Mitchell, assistant pastor at MCC who died trying to save his partner, Louis Horace Broussard. Mrs. Willie Inez Warren died with her sons, Eddie Hosea Warren and James Curtis Warren. Dr. Perry Lane Waters, Jr., a Jefferson Parish dentist died as well. Several victims were his patients and were identified by his x-rays.

When the fire broke out it left no apparent escape for those trapped in the upstairs venue. The windows were barred, and I have been told that from the street below the pastor was seen screaming while burning to death, clutching the bars that held him prisoner.

Metal bars on the windows of the Up Stairs Lounge were fourteen inches apart; while some managed to squeeze through and jump, others got stuck. That's how the MCC's pastor, Rev. Bill Larson, died, screaming, "Oh, God, no!" as the flames charred his flesh. When police and firefighters began clearing the scene, they left Larson fused to the window frame until the next morning.

On June 22, 2022, An MCC clergy Facebook page reported: "After 49 years, the City of New Orleans is finally recognizing the 32 victims of the Up Stairs Lounge arson. This Thursday at 10 am, June 23, the

City Council will hear a presentation about the fire and pass a resolution acknowledging and honoring the victims. In 1973, the tragedy was ignored by officials and ridiculed by the media. Those who died that night could have never imagined how far we've come. The actual anniversary, which is Friday, June 24th and will be marked by a ceremony at the site of the fire at 7:00 pm"

MCC LA was also torched that year on January 27, 1973. It wasn't the only time. Thankfully, no one was present in that building at the time. Arsonists set fire to other gay churches in Nashville, San Francisco, and Santa Monica in 1973-1974. On July 27, 1973, MCC San Francisco was torched. They rented space from the United Presbyterian Church; approximately $100,000 worth of damage was done. On January 15, 1974, the MCC in Santa Monica was also set on fire. Others have been vandalized and threatened in a number of ways. The pastors of the Metropolitan Community Church in Cleveland, Ohio came home one day to discover that their dog was killed and hanging lynched from a tree in their yard. But none of these horrific events could stop the move of God among His LGBT children. It kept moving forward. With every fire, like a Phoenix, it would arise from the ashes even stronger.

But historically, gay Christian people are hardly the only people who had challenges to become recognized as a part of God's fold. Church history keeps slowly progressing. God often moves to bring in other people into His family that the current Church world wants to discount, disregard and discard. Christian leaders didn't always understand what God is doing. They don't know.

Luke 9:51-56 tells the story of Jesus walking with His disciples along a dusty road on their way to Jerusalem. As they went, they entered a village of the Samaritans. Because Samaritans and the Jews of the first century were antagonistic with one another, the Samaritans would not receive Him; they were hostile toward His destination, Jerusalem. When they rejected Jesus as a guest, His disciples wanted to know whether they should call on Heaven to send down fire on Samaria to destroy it.

Jesus turned and rebuked them, and said, "You do not know what manner of spirit you are of. "For the Son of Man did not come to destroy men's lives but to save them." (*Luke 9:51-56* NKJV)

4

Though the Samaritans rejected Him initially, Jesus was still concerned about their souls. Later, in the book of Acts, A great revival took place in Samaria as Philip the evangelist shared the gospel of Christ with them. (See Acts 8) Everything has changed. God moved outside the box of His disciples' understanding.

In a similar vein, the apostle John tried to stop miracles from happening because they weren't done in the way John felt they had to happen. Outsiders from their group were performing miracles in Jesus' Name.

"We tried to stop those folks because they're not like us."

Luke 9:49

Then John answered and said, "Master, we saw someone casting out demons in Your name, and we forbade him because he does not follow with us."

That's the problem.

From the very inception of Christianity, followers have tried to identify who can join and who is excluded from the good news of the Gospel. Yet Jesus told His disciples that He had other sheep that were not in their fold, and He was going to bring them into the fold as well. He never told them what the sheep looked like, what race or sex or political party they would belong to, just that they were His.

And other sheep I have, which are not of this fold: them also I must bring, and they shall hear my voice; there shall be one-fold and one shepherd.

(*John 10:16*, KJV)

[1] Genesis 1:1-4 *The Holy Bible: New International Version*, electronic ed. (Grand Rapids: Zondervan, 1996, c1984), used by permission

[2] *ibid*

[3] Sundby, Elaine, *Calling the Rainbow People Home: A Story of Acceptance and Affirmation*, 2005

[4] http://www.gayworld.net/memorial/ (last accessed July 23, 2019)

Gays and the Gospel

Historically there have been many Christian renewals in which Biblical faith was restored. There was a promise in the book of Acts that Jesus would remain in Heaven until everything was restored as promised.

Acts 3:19-21. "Repent therefore and be converted, that your sins may be blotted out, so that times of refreshing may come from the presence of the Lord,

> 20. "and that He may send Jesus Christ, who was preached to you before,

> 21. "*whom heaven must receive until the times of restoration of all things*, which God has spoken by the mouth of all His holy prophets since the world began [1].

A few centuries after Peter spoke these words, the Christian religious world was plunged into the dark ages. The power of the early church was lost, the gifts of the Spirit listed in I Corinthians chapters 12 and 14 were almost unseen or unheard of, and salvation through faith in Christ was obliterated by a mixture of pagan rituals and a system of works.

In the 1500's Martin Luther appeared on the religious scene. He was a pious but tormented monk who could not get peace in his soul, even though he was using all the formulas available to him through a corrupt religious system. Luther knew there had to be more than paying indulgences, praying the same prayers repeatedly, humbling himself through the harsh treatment of his body, and doing good deeds. He did all this with zeal, but he still felt God was far away and angry. But one day, Martin Luther got an inspired revelation that salvation and eternal life were gifts already purchased and paid for by Christ. And by faith in the already completed works of Christ, one could be born again. It wasn't up to Martin Luther to work his way into Heaven; it was up to Luther to believe in what Christ had already provided for him as a free gift.

Martin Luther was one revivalist that God used to restore the salvation experience to the church. From the darkness of the Middle Ages, many more truths had to be restored to bring the church back to its intended power and purpose.

God keeps moving forward. In the first century, no one thought Gentiles could belong to God. Yet God used a revivalist - Peter with his rooftop experience in Acts chapter ten, as well as the Apostle Paul's ministry of opening that door to those kept outside.

Through a faulty understanding of Scripture, many first-century Jews felt Gentiles were under an irreversible curse and could not be saved unless they first became Jewish. God knocked down their misunderstanding of Scripture. Ephesians chapter 2 makes it clear that those who were once considered outsiders to the community of faith have been brought in by Jesus Himself. Jesus and the Holy Spirit are always reaching out to a wider group of humanity than Christians expect.

In a similar fashion, many have misapplied Scripture to forbid women from pastoring churches.

For centuries, prior to the 1800s, hardly anyone believed that women had a place in ministry. Yet God still has called women into ministry despite the theological prohibitions from the Southern Baptists [2] and Roman Catholic churches.

In the late 1800s, because she was a woman, Maria Woodworth-Etter initially rejected her call to ministry. She told God that she couldn't preach the gospel because her husband and sons would never allow it. Next, her sons and husband all died, and she went on the road preaching. Author Roberts Liardon calls Maria the grandmother of the Pentecostal movement that would spread across the world [3]. Signs and wonders accompanied her meetings and miraculous healings took place when she preached. But she was especially noted for bringing life and revival to churches that were dead and lifeless.

Following her, Aimee Semple McPherson became a powerhouse in the gospel. In July 1922, she opened Angelus Temple in Los Angeles. Many of Hollywood's greatest stars in her day came to hear her preach. Mary Pickford, Jean Harlow, and Clara Bow were regulars among them, and as a teenager, Anthony Quinn played in her band [4]. When she founded the Four-Square Church denomination, and its Life Bible College, on the first day one thousand pastors signed up. Her ministry was filled with healings and the winning of thousands of souls for Christ. Aimee did not waste her time with the opinions of others who thought it was against the Bible for women to preach!

After Aimee came Kathryn Kuhlman. Her radio program reached around the United States. Kuhlman's healing ministry was unparalleled for its day. Much of her public ministry would take place in auditoriums that held thousands of people. Worship would begin and while people were worshipping God, the Holy Spirit would hover over the congregation and heal people. They would run to the platform, not to be prayed for but to give God the glory and testify that a healing miracle took place. Yet today, there are still those who deny what God is doing with women in ministry. They cut that ministry option out of their churches because of their limited understanding of Scripture.

Christian textbook authors Klein, Blomberg, and Hubbard [5] note how by the same process, slavery was considered to be Biblically sanctioned by American pre-Civil War Christians. Christians have not always understood all that God was and is doing. They did not believe Gentiles were allowed into the Kingdom of God. They did not believe slavery was wrong, they did not believe women could preach, and all were based on the way they understood the Bible. They have argued over the simplest commands; whether to love their neighbor or to bash their neighbor. They don't agree about the communion table or how baptism is to be done. It comes as no surprise, then, that they have also missed out on seeing what God has been doing among the gay-affirming community.

Klein, Blomberg, and Hubbard note in their textbook that when believers study the Bible they interact with its text and Author [6].

Therefore, if God wanted to tell gay people that no matter what happened, they could never go to Heaven, as is supposed by some, then the Author of the Bible would reveal this as they interact with Him through His book. But the reality is that those conclusions are only obtained when one proof-texts the Bible. To proof-text is to pull a verse out of its context to try to prove a viewpoint.

Biblical interpretation is not all that difficult, but there are some general rules that need to be followed if one wants to understand the truths presented. In a later chapter, we will look closely at this. But to fully understand the Author's intent you have to be in a relationship with this living God. To interpret a Book written and inspired by the Holy Spirit we must be in a dynamic relationship with the Holy Spirit, in order to get His perspective on what the Spirit means for you in a text.

Over the last fifty years, gay people have been brought into this dynamic born-again experience and hearing from God for themselves. The Bible says of itself that it is alive and active (Hebrews 4:12). It is an interactive book that changes us and causes us to grow in our relationship with its Author. Jesus said that His sheep know His voice, and we know that He is a good Shepherd. He is talking to His gay children regularly. And God is telling His LGBT children that there is hope and a future for them. In fact, God has revealed a whole different plan and purpose for gays than others might think.

God began moving by His Holy Spirit in the midst of the gay community about the same time as He began moving among the youth counterculture of the 1960s. Hippies began experiencing God in a whole new way, as the Jesus movement sprung up in the late 1960s. At that time many churchgoers thought Hippies were too far gone for God to reach. Without Church help or approval, God brought them into His Kingdom anyway. Even so, many found they were not welcome in the staid and proper churches of the 1960s. As a result, all new churches sprang up, and thus many independent charismatic churches were birthed.

Simultaneously, another group found themselves being wooed by Almighty God. Gays discovered that they also were not welcome in the anti-gay conservative churches in which they had been raised. So again, all new churches were birthed beginning in the late 1960s where LGBT people and their supporters could freely worship God without fear. Thus, as noted, in October 1968, the first Metropolitan Community Church was birthed in Los Angeles. This was the first palpable openly affirming move that was evident.

However, prior to the first MCC and prior to the Stonewall Inn riots [7], there were a few attempts to organize a religious group for gay people. One such group was the Eucharistic Catholic Church of Atlanta. It was founded in 1946 by Rev. George Augustine Hyde and his spouse, Rev. John Augustine Kazantks. Their work was published in the clandestine gay press of the time and planted seeds around the nation that this reconciliation of sexuality and spirituality was possible. These groups were isolated attempts and were not connected to any other groups. But once the Stonewall riots happened, gay liberation exploded. More and more people came out of the closet, gay political organizations sprung up, and within this context, MCC churches bloomed and blossomed all over the nation and subsequently outside of the United States.

Although the Metropolitan Community Churches (MCC) were the first major sustainable gay-friendly and affirming churches on the scene, it wasn't long before many other religious groups began to appear. Dignity for Roman Catholics was one such group whose intent was to work within their established denominations to work to change the discrimination they encountered there. By 1980, Dignity already had its own building on Wealthy St. in Grand Rapids, Michigan. They were the first group to offer us a church home to rent when we started Reconciliation MCC in Grand Rapids on December 4, 1980.

Seventh Day Adventists, Episcopal, Lutheran, Methodist, Quaker, and Jewish LGBT-affirming groups all began to address the homophobia within their home congregations. Additionally, independent churches within the gay community arose as well. These church homes were needed if gay people and their supporters would ever be welcome in the family of God.

Clearly, though, it has never been God's intent to have straight churches, gay churches, black churches or white churches, or other ethnically divided churches.

Jesus said

"And other sheep I have which are not of this fold; them also I must bring, and they will hear My voice; and there will be one flock and one shepherd

John 10:16. (NKJV)

This is further stated in the New Testament in Ephesians 2:13-22

But now in Christ Jesus you who once were far off have been made near by the blood of Christ. For He Himself is our peace, who has made both one, and has broken down the middle wall of division between us, having abolished in His flesh the enmity, that is, the law of commandments contained in ordinances, so as to create in Himself one new man from the two, thus making peace, and that He might reconcile them both to God in one body through the cross, thereby putting to death the enmity. And He came and preached peace to you who were afar off and to those who were nearby. For through Him we both have access by one Spirit to the Father. Now, therefore, you are no longer strangers and foreigners, but fellow citizens with the saints and members of the household of God, having been built on the foundation of the apostles and prophets, Jesus Christ Himself being the chief cornerstone, in whom the whole building, being joined together, grows into a holy temple in the Lord, in whom you also are being built together for a habitation of God in the Spirit.[8]

When the Charismatic movement began in the late 1960s and early 1970's Charismatic gatherings began to surface in the largest stadiums in America. One pinnacle gathering took place at the Arrowhead Stadium in Kansas City in July 1977. Over 50,000 Charismatic Christians gathered under the various banners and streams of that flow. Messianic Jews worshipped alongside Roman Catholics, and alongside Assembly of God leadership. All streams were present as far as the organizers knew. Yet, the most remarkable thing that happened in the midst of this flow of worship was a prophecy that came forth: "to mourn...weep...for the body of My Son is broken [9]."

The organizers of the conference felt that meant to have an even bigger conference with more people invited. So, the next year a conference was held in New York City with 100,000 people in attendance.

God was clearly grieved that His Son's body was actually broken, not merely just needing to come together for a meeting. By this time the Jesus movement had been incorporated and accepted into the Charismatic movement, but gay Christians were neither acknowledged, nor received. They were still demonized as heretics. The New York conference did not bring any further healing or wholeness to the body than it had in Kansas City.

But the more the Holy Spirit began to work as a fresh new move of God with His LGBT children; the former move had a visceral and yet organized opposition. This became the most noted and publicized when Miami-Dade County in Florida passed an anti-discrimination, gay-affirming ordinance. Anita Bryant, at the time, was gaining more and more fame as a singer and television personality. She had a contract with the Florida Citrus Commission and sang in their commercials. A famous slogan they used was that "A Day without orange juice was a day without sunshine". Bryant strongly objected to gay people having legal protections and began a campaign called *Save our Children* to remove the ordinance from the law by a referendum. She spouted that gay teachers were all pedophiles who recruit children into homosexuality. Her rationale was that since they could not reproduce, they had to increase their numbers by recruiting and seducing children into their lair. The name of the campaign had to be changed to "Protect America's Children" because of legal action by the Save the Children foundation.

On June 7, 1977, Bryant's campaign led to a repeal of the anti-discrimination ordinance by a margin of 69 to 31 percent. This emboldened her to take on other such anti-discrimination laws around the nation. Jerry Falwell joined in her crusade. On the night before the vote in Florida, I was in Pittsburgh. In MCC Pittsburgh, we had a gay Christian man named Joseph Houle who played guitar and led in worship. MCC Pittsburgh gathered at his home that night. We knew the seriousness of this ordinance in Florida. If it was overturned, it could erase all legal gains we had made thus far. We fasted all that day and came to Joe's house to worship and pray. We prayed hard and long.

Finally, the Holy Spirit gave me a word to share. He said, "Don't worry about this." But when the next day the vote went against gays, I didn't know what to think. So, we just waited to see what God would do, and be patient.

Though Anita Bryant got the victory for the ordinance being overturned, she really lost the battle. Her vitriolic attitude caused many entertainers to come to our side. Bryant became the butt of many jokes and ridicule. Even late-night shows like Johnny Carson and Saturday Night Live made fun of her. She became a liability, and the Florida Citrus Commission dropped her as their spokesperson. In February 1977, the Singer Corporation canceled an offer to sponsor an upcoming television show because of the "extensive national publicity arising from her controversial political activities."[10]

On October 14, 1977, Bryant was hit with a pie thrown at her by Thom L. Higgins. Bryant was on television when this happened and she responded, "At least it's a fruit pie."[11] She then began to pray for God to forgive him "for his deviant lifestyle" then she began crying, still on the camera. Her victory at the polls caused an immediate backlash. Around the nation, gay bars and other supporters boycotted orange juice. You wouldn't be seen drinking that! With these cancellations, her career began to plummet. Then her marriage fell apart and in 1980 she divorced her husband, Bob Green. The unforgiving fundamentalist church world would not forgive her for divorce. More and more church events were canceled. Her reputation plummeted from a wholesome Christian mother to a self-righteous bigot. The ordinance she had repealed in Florida was reinstated 30 years later, on November 25, 2008, when the Miami-Dade Circuit Courts declared the discriminational law unconstitutional.

Then finally, in 2021, Bryant's granddaughter, Sarah Green, came out publicly as a lesbian by announcing her pending marriage to a woman. She stated, however, that she was having difficulty deciding whether she should invite her grandmother to the ceremony.[12]

Way back on the hot June night in 1977 before the vote, we prayed. We asked God to intervene. Over and over God kept showing us how much He loves us and how much He will protect us from those who would hurt us.

Yet, gays were still outsiders to the larger Body of Christ. And so were the rare non-gay churches that cared about their gay members. On May 5, 2003, Ken Garfield, the Religion Editor of the *Charlotte Observer* reported in an ongoing story [13] that McGill Baptist Church was kicked out of the Cabarrus Baptist Association because they baptized two gay men. McGill, a century-old Concord North Carolina church of 800 members was notified that the Cabarrus association of 81 Southern Baptist churches voted overwhelmingly to sever their ties with McGill. The two baptized gay men had been partners for six years and found God's love in that church. But the Southern Baptist Association found no love for the men or the church that baptized them.

The Rev. Randy Wadford, the association's mission director, read a statement after the vote in which he said "the homosexual lifestyle is contrary to God's will and plan for mankind. ... To allow individuals into the membership of a local church without evidence or testimony of true repentance is to condone the old lifestyle." Garfield reported.[14]

Garfield also reported that

"While believing in the Christian tenet that all are sinners in need of God's forgiveness, the gay couple from McGill doesn't believe their relationship makes them sinners".[15]

Why would these gay men even think their relationship was sinful? God has been moving in the hearts and minds of His children to reveal His heart on the matter. Though the Cabarrus Baptist Association believed the men were sinning because they were still in a loving relationship, it is their faulty interpretation of scripture that leads them and many others to this conclusion. But God knows how to work in the human heart to convince us of wrongdoing. These believers have no twinge in their consciences that the love and home they share is a sin.

Evangelical Author Tony Campolo told a powerful story at a talk at North Park College Chapel on February 29, 1996. He said:

...Let me tell you a story. I have a friend. He pastored a church up in Brooklyn. It was a dying community, a place where everything was disintegrating. He kept his family and himself fed and cared for by doing odd jobs, one of which was doing funerals for the local undertaker when nobody else would take them. The man was a saint, and he didn't know it, so I would call him and get great stories because he never used them. And I would always say, Jim, anything good happens that I can tell, any good story that, anything happens this week?

He'd always say no.

"What about Tuesday at 11 o'clock? What were you doing then?" "Oh, he said, that was fascinating. The undertaker called me early in the morning because he had a man to bury who had died of AIDS and nobody wanted to take the funeral, so I ended up taking the funeral."

I said, "What was it like?

He said, "About 25 homosexual men came and sat there. Never once, Tony, did they ever look up at me. The whole time I spoke their heads were down and they were looking at the floor. Never once did they ever make eye contact with me during the funeral. We went out and got in some cars and we followed the hearse out to the cemetery and lowered the body into the grave. I stood on one side of the grave. These twenty-five homosexual men are on the other side. Standing there like statues, neither looking to the right nor to the left, looking straight out into infinity. Never budging just sitting there, standing there rigid like statues. I read some scripture. I said some prayers. I committed the body to the grave. I said the benediction and I started to move - walk away, but they didn't move. They stood there as though frozen so I, so I came back and I said, 'Excuse me, is there anything else I can do?'

"And one of the men said, 'Yes. I never go to church. Used to go to church but I don't go to church. The only thing I really liked about church was when they read from the Bible, especially King James. I like the King James. You didn't read the 23rd psalm. I thought they always read that at funerals. Could you read the 23rd Psalm?'"

Jim opened the Bible and read the 23rd Psalm. Another man said, "There's a passage in the 3rd chapter of John about being born again. I like that passage."

John read that. Then a third man said, "The 8th chapter of Romans, right at the end, that's what keeps me going."

And Jim read to these homosexual men. "Neither height nor depth, neither principalities nor powers, neither things present nor things to come, nothing, nothing can separate us from the love of God which is in Christ Jesus our Lord."

Nothing. And when he told me that, I hurt, I hurt, because I knew that these men wanted to hear the Bible but would never step foot inside a church because they are convinced that church people despise them. And do you know why they think church people despise them?

Because church people despise them.[16]

So, all in all, it had to be a move of the Holy Spirit to bring gay people and their allies into the Kingdom of God with a message that God loves us. Primarily because the church world refused to even consider such a thing possible. For the most part, many church groups and conservative denominations actively fight any progress for gay rights with their pocketbooks, their votes, and legislation. They believe God is on their side. But God has been moving and actively engaged in bringing His LGBT children into His house.

In the 1970s there were three streams flowing simultaneously. Among them were the Jesus movement, in which counterculture, Hippie young people were coming to Christ in the thousands; the Charismatic movement, in which quiet, dry liturgical denominations were being infused with the Holy Spirit: Catholics, Lutherans, and Episcopalians were getting filled with the Holy Spirit. And finally, so were gay people. Simultaneously, during these three streams, was the sexual revolution. The moral code of the 1950s was being rejected by the young people of the 1970s. Free love without commitment was easy to find. Because of the revolt against the police and oppression begun by the Stonewall Inn riots in New York, gays became more open and demanded rights and liberation. But the church world would have none of it, nor would they support gays. They set themselves up as our enemies. That left gay people with no moral compass, and we found ourselves more likely allies with the free love philosophy. Gay sexual liaisons were available pretty much anytime. The Holy Spirit raised up churches for the LGBT community within this atmosphere. We knew we were a part of the Body of Christ, but just not accepted as such by the rest of the Body. All these streams were flowing over their banks, and you'd be likely to run into someone from all of them on any particular day.

Just before I discovered MCC in Pittsburgh, PA, in 1975, I was a student at the University of Pittsburgh, and sitting at McDonald's when one of my high school peers walked in. Nancy walked up and sat down at my table. I knew her, but not really well, though I always liked her. We didn't run in the same circles in high school, so I didn't know very much about her. She was now in the flow of the Charismatic Movement. She immediately began to testify about Jesus. She told me how she used to date married men when she was in high school, but then she found Jesus. She realized her sexual promiscuity was immoral and now she was married to Jesus alone. Since I didn't respond to her testimony, after a few more minutes she left. I thought, poor Nancy! I didn't see anything wrong with having fun with married men and figured she now had a religious crutch. But I figured if she's happy, that's alright for her. I was oblivious to what she was talking about.

Then I found MCC in Pittsburgh and discovered Jesus for myself. He was truly the Lover of my soul. Our Pastor, Rev. Frank Scott had an altar call in January 1975, and I went forward. He used the words "making a commitment to Christ." That's what I did.

Because I was openly gay, I figured I could do what I wanted in terms of my sexual orientation. I wasn't going to worry anymore about heterosexual condemnation. I got myself a few dolls with which to decorate my apartment because I liked them. And when I dated girls in high school, I sometimes bought them perfume as a gift. I liked Chanel #5. So, I thought, I like that, so I will buy myself some. I was a militant activist on my campus. I figured if my wearing women's perfume made people think I'm gay, what of it, I am! I went to my next class proudly wearing my recently purchased Chanel #5. I sat down next to a friend in the large auditorium.

She turned to me and emphatically said, "Good Lord, you smell like a bordello!"

That completely embarrassed me. I wasn't expecting that. I never wore it again, and finally gave it as a gift to another female friend.

Then one day I noticed the clothes my dolls were wearing needed washed. I went to the nearby laundromat and threw in the doll clothes with my regular laundry. In came one of the Christians, like Nancy, who felt the need to get people saved. On her grey wool coat, she had a huge red button that said GET SMART, GET SAVED. I knew the Christian community rejected us, and at minimum would expect us to repent of our so-called sin of homosexuality, and they can be pretty confrontational about it. I was in no mood to deal with her. Of course, she walked up to me and said that I needed to get saved. She was aggressive. I now realized that I would be in for a real confrontation once I pulled the doll's clothes out of the dryer. Finally, she got me angry enough, that I blurted out, "I don't need to get saved, I already made a commitment to Christ, and I am very happy with my church."

She asked, "You made a commitment to Christ?"

I said "Yes!"

"Well, then, you are saved." She declared.

"I am? " I asked.

"Yes." She said. Then she left.

This made me very happy because I didn't know that the two terms meant the same thing and that I was also saved. It also made me happy because I could now take my doll clothes out of the dryer to fold them.

[1] *The Holy Bible: New King James Version*, electronic ed. (Thomas Nelson ©1982), used by permission

[2] *SBC Moves To Limit Office Of Pastor To Men*, The Christian Century 117 no18 641 Je 7-14 2000

[3] Roberts Liardon, *God's Generals, Why They Succeeded and Why Some Failed,* Tulsa, OK, Albury Publishing, 1996, pg. 47

[4] Ibid., p. 255

[5] William W. Klein, Craig L. Blomberg, and Robert L. Hubbard *Introduction to Biblical Interpretation* Nashville, TN, Thomas Nelson Publishers, 2004, p 12

[6] Ibid. p 166

[7] June 28, 1969, The New York City police raided the Stonewall Inn, a gay club located in Greenwich Village in New York City. Riots ensued among bar patrons and neighborhood residents as police hauled employees and patrons out of the bar. This led to six days of protests and clashes with law enforcement. This is typically noted as the beginning of the Gay Pride Movement.

[8] Ephesians 2:13-22 (NKJV)

[9] Stanley Burgess and Gary B. McGee, Editors, *Dictionary of Pentecostal and Charismatic Movements*, Grand Rapids, MI, Zondervan Publishing House, 1988, p. 139

[10] "Gay Rights Dispute Stops Bryant's Show". The Washington Post. *Retrieved June 23, 2022.*

[11] "CNN Transcripts". Transcripts.cnn.com. April 26, 2008. *Retrieved June 23, 2022*

[12] ^ "Another Pie in the Face for Anita Bryant: Her Granddaughter Is Gay". Advocate.com. July 27, 2021. Last accessed June 22, 2022 https://www.advocate.com/people/2021/7/27/another-pie-face-anita-bryant-her-granddaughter-gay

[13] http://www.charlotte.com/mld/observer/news/local/5787403.htm (last accessed June 24, 2005)

[14] Ibid.

[15] Ibid.

[16] http://www.bridges-across.org/ba/campolo.htm (last accessed January 19, 2007)

AIDS and the Miracles

During the same time as the Christian movement was exploding among the gay community, a new plague was surfacing. The anti-gay religious rhetoric was quick to call AIDS the *gay plague* and identify it as God's judgment on the gay community.

Yet in the midst of this tragedy came many examples of God's love and caring.

Rev. Steve Pieters is now a retired minister with the Metropolitan Community Churches. He was one of the first people to have AIDS in the early days of the disease and yet God kept giving him life, not death. Rev. Pieters wrote in July 1996

"Your mission," my doctor told me after my AIDS diagnosis in 1984, "is to stay alive long enough for us to find a way to make the virus manageable, to make it stop destroying the immune system." And I have lived to see that day.[1]

His personal story was one of hope and inspiration.

The Rev. Dr. A. Stephen Pieters is a long-term survivor of AIDS. Diagnosed with AIDS-related complex (ARC) in 1982, and AIDS/ Kaposi's Sarcoma and Lymphoma in 1984, his remarkable story of re-covery serves as an inspiring example of healing and hope. Rev. Pieters was one of twelve invited guests at a Prayer Breakfast at the White House with U.S. President Bill Clinton, Vice President Al Gore, and National AIDS Policy Coordinator Kristine Gebbie prior to World AIDS Day 1993. The President talked about Rev. Pieters in his World AIDS Day speech on December 1, 1993.

He has been interviewed by the *Los Angeles Sunday Times*, *Time* magazine, *Omni* magazine, *Life* magazine, and numerous television talk and news shows including CNN, Headline News, Tammy's House Party (starring Tammy Faye Bakker), CBS This Morning, the Tom Snyder Show, America Talks Back, and Real Life with Jane Pauley. He was a featured speaker at an entertainment industry dinner benefit for AIDS Project Los Angeles (APLA), given by Elizabeth Taylor and honoring former First Lady Betty Ford. In November 1987 he presented the Buddy of the Year Award to Whoopi Goldberg at APLA's third annual entertainment industry benefit. In the summer of 1990, he appeared as himself in the hit play, "AIDS US/II." His story also appears in the books, *Surviving AIDS* by Michael Callen, *Voices That Care* by Neal Hitchens, and *Don't Be Afraid Anymore* by Rev. Troy D. Perry.[2]

Rev. Pieters was a featured guest on *Tammy's House Party* television program in 1985, the days when Tammy Faye Bakker hosted it. The powerful 1985 TV program with Tammy Faye Bakker can be seen on YouTube.[3] In it, Rev. Pieters broke down barriers. The Holy Spirit was clearly evident. This powerful interview was a game changer. Tammy interviewed Rev. Pieters and asked pertinent questions that non-gay Christians had about AIDS and gay people. Rev. Pieters answered with such grace and love and intelligence that in the end, Tammy was crying and said she just wanted to hug Steve. He had to have the interview via satellite from California since at the time he was undergoing chemo treatments and couldn't join her on the set in Heritage USA, South Carolina. Tammy went on to say that love was the bottom line and that all Christians should be able to reach out to people with AIDS and give them the love of God. Well, instead, she got a lot of flak and hate mail for having a homosexual with AIDS on her program.

Rev. Craig Franklin of Grace Fellowship in Christ Jesus in Dallas Texas was another one who testified of God's grace and hope. I heard him testify of a time when, because of HIV, he was overrun with an opportunistic parvovirus, commonly infecting canines. His doctors didn't know what to do and gave up hope. Yet he stood before us healthy and whole testifying that it was only God who brought him through. He is still, in 2022, a living testimony to the power of God in his life.

Paul Henderson was a member of our church in the 1980s. He was in his 50's, though, he'd never admit to an actual age. Paul loved music and was an accomplished musician. He had a grand piano and a church organ in his living room. On my visits to his home, he often would record himself playing the organ, then hit PLAY and get on his piano and play along. He taught our church so many wonderful worship songs. It broke my heart when he found out he was HIV positive because, at that time, it was almost a certain death sentence. Thousands had died of this disease and its complications. As we feared, one day Paul came down with an infection. Having been a veteran during the Korean War, he was admitted to the Dayton Ohio Veteran's Hospital. I went to see him, and it was clear that the infection had attacked his brain. Paul was completely incoherent. He could not care for himself, feed himself, walk or even talk. He was a zombie glued to his bed.

Nonetheless, we believed God loves us and answers our prayers. I laid hands on his head and prayerfully demanded that his mind be restored in the name of Jesus!

It was a few days before I could get back to the hospital to see Paul. When I did, his bed was empty, and I thought the worse! I figured he died. I went to the nurses' station to ask what ever happened to Paul Henderson. She told me he went down the hall to take a shower. His faculties had been completely restored and he was once again in his right mind. Paul lived many years after that, and when you visited him, you could hear that piano and organ singing God's praises.

Then there is the story of Rev. Chuck Breckenridge.

Pastor Chuck Breckenridge came to us from Springfield Illinois. He first contacted us and let us know that he was available to hold a revival for us if we'd like. It was a win-win situation. He was young and talented, he could sing, preach, play piano and organ, and thus he held our first revival meeting. His organization, Sonshine Evangelistic Team, came under the auspices of Community Gospel Church in Dayton at our January 1989 Board meeting. He said this church in Ohio was where God wanted him, so he was moving to Dayton. We financially helped him move in April of that year. All of us were excited that he was coming. Though we had a co-pastorate with Bill Roberts and me, we ultimately took on Chuck as an Associate pastor. Over the next few years, Rev. Bill Roberts moved to Portland Oregon to pastor the church that Naomi Harvey had started, and Chuck moved on to Tulsa Oklahoma, and has pastored Diversity Christian Church [4] since he founded it in June of 2000. During his time with us, Chuck let us know that he was HIV positive. He maintained good health while he was with us, but as he posted several times on his Facebook page, he faced near death in a coma in 2007.

As Pastor Chuck Breckenridge wrote on Facebook on 8-7-2021:

My closing thought...

I worked all day today...over 12 hours...although not manual labor it still worked. Before that began, I had a doctor's appointment this morning with my ID doctor.

Most of you know in October of 2007 I was in the hospital with PCP pneumonia ...my CD4 count was 48... and I was in the hospital on a vent for 11 days in a medically induced coma with a 1% chance of survival.

....an experience neither I nor my friends and family will forget.

Today my viral load was undetectable and my CD4 count is 918...not where I would like it but a long way from 48.

I went from 1% chance of survival to working full-time realtor and full-time pastor (I don't believe either of those can be part-time).

Tonight, as I was finishing up work Violet and Jasmine were playing and getting a little loud...right before I started to tell them to quieten down, I realized how beautiful that sound was. I was reminded I'm still here to hear those sounds.

As tired as I may get tonight, I am simply thankful to still be here...this year was quite the year ... we lost a lot ... but in the midst of losing some things, we found some things also. I love this song that we sing...

You ask me how it is that I'm still standing.

You wonder how I made it through the storm?

I don't boast of any special powers,

There's no secret I just kept holding on.

I held on till the storm was over, I don't claim to be a hero,

I don't have all the answers I held on, till the storm was over,

not because I'm good, not because I'm great, not because I'm strong...I held on.

Whatever you may be facing tonight .... when you have done all to stand ... just stand ... He will speak to your storm; He will calm the winds and the waves, and He will bring peace ... I don't talk about this because I have heard about it but because I have experienced it ... I have special connections ... I know the master of the wind![5]

Not everyone was healed but we saw miracles, nonetheless. That reminded me of Cory. He was a gay man who I had as a patient when I did home health care. Cory had AIDS. His spouse was a dentist in the military, and I often would visit with them both as I came to take care of Cory's physical nursing needs. They had a lovely romantic relationship. Cory had been an antique dealer in New York City and decided at some point to open a shop in Paris, France instead. It was there in Paris, that he met Dave, the dentist who would become his lover and friend. Dave told me one day that he was so discouraged. Cory kept getting sicker, and Dave said he hoped one day their love life could be restored and go beyond coming home to change another diaper. Cory was finally hospitalized, and I visited him and Dave at the hospital bedside frequently. Then it was Christmas Eve. I visited with them both and asked Cory about his relationship with Christ. It was obvious he didn't have much time left. Cory seemed annoyed and demanded "Pastor Sam, what exactly do you want me to do?!"

I told him I wanted him to become a Christian by trusting in Jesus as his Lord and Savior. With a sigh, Corrie said, "Alright, then!"

As we prayed, and Cory sincerely asked Christ into his heart, you could see a change take place. A lightness came, the heaviness was removed, and his face began to shine. Dave, already a Christian, was crying. On Christmas day, Cory went to celebrate Jesus' birthday with Him in person as he slipped into eternity. No one could tell us God hates gays! We saw Him love them right into Heaven way too many times.

[1] http://www.mccgham.org/?cat=10 (last accessed August 28, 2009)

[2] http://www.thebody.com/content/art39714.html (last accessed August 28, 2009)

[3] The 1985 interview with Tammy Faye: https://youtu.be/GjXXdQ6VceQ (last accessed June 21, 2022)

[4] http://realacceptance.com/ last accessed August 3, 2022

[5] 8-7-2021 Pastor Chuck Breckenridge's Facebook page.

Early Pioneers

Rev. Troy Perry

No one can tell the story of the gay Christian movement without telling the story of the father and founder of the movement. Rev. Troy Perry is the catalyst and point person God used to open this locked harvest field.

In the early 1960s Troy Perry had been a Pentecostal minister, married with children, who realized he was gay, and then shared that information with his wife. That was the end of the ministry as he knew it. A divorce and defrocking ensued. By 1968, Troy was convinced God no longer loved him, and after a failed relationship with a man named Benny, Perry attempted suicide using a razor blade on his wrists.[1] With the help of neighbors, Benny found Perry in time to rescue him. The next thing Perry knew he was in a Los Angeles emergency room. Because he didn't die as expected, he began to get insight from God; especially through Christians and friends who cared about him and were bold enough to speak into his life. Eventually, even though he was a gay minister, God laid it on his heart to do the impossible - start a church where all God's children would be welcome; gays, lesbians, transgender folks, bisexuals, straights - really anyone. He started Metropolitan Community Church (MCC) in his living room on October 6, 1968.

The Lord had to do a lot of speaking to get Troy to understand such a thing was even possible. One of the people God used was his own Christian mother. As he tells the story:

During this time of planning and preparing, I was such a happy individual. Willie Smith (Perry's roommate) saw me walking around the house humming, smiling, and full of energy. He nailed me about it one day.

He said, "What's eating on you?

So, I leveled with him. I said, "Well, Willie I'm sure that God wants me to start a new church."

Willie just collapsed and said, "Oh, my God, I thought you were over all that silliness."

I said, "Wait a minute, Willie. This is a church for us, it will serve the homosexuals, the gay community."

Well, Willie thought that was crazy. He said, "You mean you really are serious about this religious stuff?"

I assured him that I was. I said, "I know, Willie, that it's the thing to do. I've got to try and see if I can't bring a message, God's message, to all the gay people."

What Willie wanted to know was this: "How are you going to organize a bunch of queens, and get them to follow any religion or any person, or do anything together? You know how bitchy we are. We always act individually. Nobody has ever organized the gay community into anything and accomplished anything. It's ridiculous."

I told Willie I would go ahead anyway. "And" I added, "we'll do it right here."

Willie was horrified.

He said, "You've got to be kidding. I'm already too much for Huntington Park. And you're going to have all those faggots from Hollywood down here running in and out of our house to attend church services? The neighborhood just can't take the strain!"

He just looked at me again, and said, "Okay. If you're going to do it, go ahead. But don't be too disappointed if it doesn't happen. Helping queens get religion isn't anybody's bag."

Then he added, "But if it does work...count me in."

So, I asked Lee Glaze, owner of The Patch gay bar, about it. Lee thought it would be just great. I asked him what he thought was the best way to reach the gay community. He thought it over.

While he was thinking, I said, "I'm going to advertise it in The Advocate, I guess. What do you think about it?"

He said, "That's a great idea. As a matter of fact, it happens that the editor of The Advocate and his lover are here in The Patch tonight. Would you like to meet them?"

I was eager to, so I went into Lee's side office near the bar. He brought in Dick and Bill and made the introductions. We started talking and I explained my plans. They were skeptical about what I was trying to do. Was this some kind of business venture? Just what was I up to? They weren't sure that they wanted to sell me any advertising at all. So, I really gave them my pitch. And when we finished, they not only took the ad, but they also gave me a good rate on it. They also told me that they might, just might, even attend a service at Metropolitan Community Church (MCC), if it ever got started.

Now at that time, The Advocate was published only once a month. I decided I would advertise in the October issue which would hit the street the last week of September. So, I set the date for my first service. It was October 6, 1968. I had about two weeks between the publication of the first ad and the first worship service.

Just about ten days before the first service, my mother came down to see me. She and her husband were separating, and she was going to go back home to Florida for a vacation. She knew of my suicide attempt, of course, and she kept much closer contact with me. I visited her as frequently as I could.

Again, I'm going to have her tell, in her own words; something of the way she saw it.

"One day, I visited with Troy at his home in Huntington Park. He seemed kind of distracted and I was afraid that he was losing interest in his faith, in any kind of church or religion. And we were talking. I said to him, 'Troy, have you ever thought about starting a church?' Well, that stunned him. I guess I must have really read his mind. But we were talking, and he told me that a friend of his had been arrested -- busted as they call it -- on some kind of homosexual charge or other.

And he told how much that boy needed help. And I said to Troy, 'Well, haven't you ever thought about starting a church for homosexuals?' Well, a change came over him, and he looked at me and that was it. He said that that was just what he had been praying about and that was what he was going to do. He looked so fierce and intent. He said that it had been uppermost in his mind for several weeks."[2]

I came into MCC in 1975 and stayed for eleven years. I knew it was a powerful move of God. Gay folks were coming to Christ in droves, with churches springing up faster than anyone could count. In God's timing, this move was working simultaneously with the Charismatic Movement.

It grew so rapidly that it quickly became the largest LGBT-affirming organization in the world. It seemed overnight that they grew to hundreds of congregations and were found in thirty-seven [3] nations, including places like Tanzania. That first service had 12 people. The next week there were 16. But in a short time, more than 43,000 people consider themselves members or adherents of Metropolitan Community churches.

Rev. Troy Perry's story is well documented in several books, including his own books: *The Lord is my Shepherd and He knows I'm Gay [4]* (June 1987) and also *Don't Be Afraid Anymore: The Story of Reverend Troy Perry and the Metropolitan Community Churches* [5] (March 1992)

I first met Rev. Troy Perry in 1975. I had been the president of Gay Students at Pitt, at the University of Pittsburgh, and in 1975 we were hosting a Human Sexuality Conference on campus. My predecessor had organized the entire event many months before I walked into the organization, so I merely inherited a conference that was already pre-programmed. Famous speakers were lined up, such as Elaine Noble, the first person elected to a political office as an open lesbian. Another speaker was Rita May Brown, the author of *Ruby Fruit Jungle [6]*. But so was this Rev. Troy Perry from Los Angeles. I had never heard of him and felt put off that a minister would be coming to talk to gay people. I had never heard a positive message towards gays and was leery of what this guy might say. As president of the sponsoring organization, I felt obligated to go and was surprised by how inspiring, upbeat, and passionate this minister spoke. I was mesmerized. I was a fish in the gay pond that had just been caught. After his talk, Troy introduced me to Rev. Frank Scott, the founder of a new MCC in Pittsburgh, Pennsylvania. The church was only a few weeks old. It took me a few weeks to get the courage to go, but go I did. I thought what better place to meet a potential spouse than in a gay church? What I found was not a man, but a living Savior, Jesus, the Son of God. I was saved and filled with the Holy Spirit in that first year.

Frank Scott had been a Charismatic Baptist pastor but was kicked out when his gay orientation was discovered. He was full of life and brought that life with him as the pastor of this new church. I felt like a sponge that had been in a desert for a hundred years and had discovered a trickle of living water flowing past me. I could not soak up enough of this living water. I was there every time the church doors were opened. I knew many gay people from the various political organizations in Pittsburgh's gay community and had to tell them all; "You have got to get to this church! You won't believe how wonderful it is!"

I was sold; hook line and sinker on Jesus, MCC, and church.

In the summer of 1976, during the USA's bicentennial, the Universal Fellowship of Metropolitan Community Churches was having its annual international conference in Washington D.C. Several of us from Pittsburgh were going. I was a fairly poor college student at the time and didn't have the resources to attend, but the MCC folks in Washington opened their homes and hearts and I was given free housing in Washington for the week. At the registration table, they gave all conference attendees a tote bag. It included your registration materials; the agenda for the week, certainly, but it also included a gay magazine telling you where all the gay bars were in Washington, and last but not least a great big yellow smiley face button that said HAVE A GAY DAY. My friend Joe Smith and I were staying in the same home, and we walked together to the church conference location through DC's streets. Joe was fairly effeminate and very expressive if I must say so myself, and he was swinging that plastic bag by its handles as if he had a new purse. Suddenly a man came running up behind us at great speed. He grabbed Joe's bag and ran off down the street. At first, we were shocked realizing we'd just been robbed! But then we started laughing hysterically as we pictured the man looking into his thieving take and saw that huge yellow HAVE A GAY DAY button and a map of DC gay bars!

Rev. Frank Scott, my first pastor and the man who led me into the baptism of the Holy Spirit, eventually left the pulpit in Pittsburgh and headed across the Atlantic. After he pastored in Bournemouth, UK, he became responsible for new churches in Southampton, Bath, and Exeter, England. This move of God just kept expanding.

Over the next eleven years, I stayed with MCC and became a student clergy within their ranks. I was licensed as a clergy in 1981. By then I had been in MCC churches in Pittsburgh, Pennsylvania; Phoenix, Arizona, and then Detroit, Michigan. It was in Detroit that my call to ministry began to take shape. It was under the mentorship of Rev. Brenda Hunt of MCC Detroit, that I began my ministerial training. I dated a man in Detroit who was from Grand Rapids, Michigan, and one weekend we made a trip there. That started the birth of a church in my spirit in Grand Rapids. We had gone to a party of his friends, mostly gay men, and as I watched these guys interact with each other, it was obvious they could use a church. So, with my local church's prayers and blessing, I began commuting from Detroit to Grand Rapids Michigan, and Reconciliation MCC was birthed in December of 1980.

Rev. Elder Troy Perry was coming to Detroit along with all the other Elders of the fellowship for a Minister's conference held in a wooded campground setting outside of Detroit. They were then going to be available to preach in nearby and local churches. I wanted Troy Perry to come to the little MCC church I had founded in Grand Rapids

Michigan. But my colleague, another student clergy, Lin Stoner, won out and got him to preach in Flint, Michigan, at Redeemer MCC. I was given the opportunity to have two Elders rather than one. I would take Rev. Elder John Hose and Rev. Elder Freda Smith with me to Reconciliation MCC in Grand Rapids. I was, however, requested to be the one to pick up Rev. Troy at the Detroit Metropolitan Airport.

At this point, I need to interject. At the time the affirming churches and movement began, gays had no previous church home, we were vehemently not welcome. Nor did we have any role models. Gay folks, for the most part, had their own subculture, hidden from the mainstream. Gay men and lesbians met primarily through gay bars, or through friends in a social circle of like-minded people. The men also had bathhouses and known cruising areas in which to meet for a quick sexual encounter. It was a social culture of secretive liaisons that were often very short-lived. Promiscuity was an accepted and expected lifestyle then. So, when churches sprang up, the biggest message that needed to be conveyed was that God did not hate us and we too, could be Heaven bound through the sacrifice of Jesus on the cross, and faith in Him. The primary message was God loves you, just as you are. The sexual promiscuity issue was not addressed and still was heavily part of the culture. One example of this prevalent attitude was an interview given by Rev. Larry Bernier. He too was a leading minister in MCC and was the founder of several MCC churches on both coasts. He was quoted as saying that he had "no conflict for him in worshipping Jesus at service and then running out to have anonymous sex in the shrubs at the Fenway" (Boston, MA) [7]

It wasn't until AIDS came on the scene in the early 1980s that people began to see that promiscuity was not prudent. In 1977 as a member of the Metropolitan Community Church of Pittsburgh, PA, I wanted to marry the man I loved. His name was Clyde. Marriage was not legal, so MCC provided Holy Unions, a spiritual joining before the church and friends. Prior to our wedding, we had a counseling session with Pastor Frank Scott and his spouse Rev. Cliff Turpin. One of the first questions they asked in that session was how we will deal with infidelity in our relationship. I said I didn't expect any. Cliff said, "Oh it will happen, alright. It always does." Well, in this case, he was right. Clyde had many secret sexual liaisons when I would be at work. It ended our relationship after three years. Clyde also died of AIDS.

As the Holy Spirit continued to work with His LGBT children, little by little we began to understand that God's standards were the same for us as for His heterosexual children. The new expectation was that we would be faithful to the partner we had committed to, and not be unfaithful. This took a while to become the new normal among the gay Christian community. Women as well as men would hook up and break up and start the cycle again, even among leadership. Lesbians tended to stay together a little longer, though. Yet lust was often still a primary motivator for relationships. So, it was for me during this time when Troy was coming to Detroit.

I was a single young gay man still in my twenties when I was asked to pick up Rev. Perry at the Detroit Metropolitan Airport. For some carnal reason, possibly to get him to really notice me (I hardly remember anymore), I decided to take off my underwear and meet him wearing my tight blue jeans. (This is stupid, I know). Nonetheless, I changed in my pastor's office and since she had a stack of brown paper bags available for trash bags, I slipped off my white briefs, or "whitey-tighties" as they were called and placed them in an available brown bag.

As the gay Christian movement began to blossom, only the Holy Spirit could mentor us. There was no other mentor. If we looked to the world for counsel among our peers, the world order was getting turned upside down. Sex, drugs, Rock and Roll; free love, and Woodstock, were the examples we saw among the youth of our day. It was all over our college campuses. If we looked to the church, we were not given advice; we were given the left boot of fellowship. We were cast out and humiliated. After a private conversation with our heterosexual church pastors, our families were phoned, and we were outed. Or we were brought before the church to have the "homosexual demon" cast out of us. That didn't work. They couldn't drive out a demon that wasn't there. It drove us out of the church.

We looked to the church for a moral compass; they never offered one. They never imagined that we also watched the newly budding Christian television programs. But we were the objects of hatred in sermons even there. Instead of learning faith, we learned loathing and disgust. Preachers freely declared that AIDS, the "gay plague" was proof of God's judgment against us, and that God hated us. So often it seemed preachers had two favorite topics: abortion and homosexuality. We always got top billing. It was quickly discovered that the more a preacher railed against the evils of homosexuality running rampant in our culture, and especially how we were destroying the family, the more their ministry financially flourished. Focus on the Family with James Dobson, and Jerry Falwell grew wealthy and politically influential by slandering gays week after week on their programs. If we were to learn what holiness looked like for LGBT Christian people, only the Holy Spirit could be our guide. But it is no surprise that the Holy Spirit was and is up to the task. He was working on me. So, I was still as carnal as the next guy. I still had a lot to learn; of course, I still do.

In the book of Revelation, chapter 2 vs 18-23 we see the church of Thyatira being addressed:

'These things says the Son of God, who has eyes like a flame of fire, and His feet like fine brass: **19** "I know your works, love, service, faith, and your patience; and *as* for your works, the last *are* more than the first. **20** Nevertheless I have a few things against you because you allow that woman Jezebel, who calls herself a prophetess, to teach and seduce My servants to commit sexual immorality and eat things sacrificed to idols. **21** And I gave her time to repent of her sexual immorality, and she did not repent. **22** Indeed I will cast her into a sickbed, and those who commit adultery with her into great tribulation unless they repent of their deeds. **23** I will kill her children with death, and all the churches shall know that I am He who searches the minds and hearts. And I will give to each one of you according to your works.

The woman addressed as Jezebel would have had a demonic spirit influencing her, by the same name. It would also be the same spirit that influenced the ancient Queen Jezebel of Israel in 1 Kings 19. This spirit hates the prophetic voice and attempts to discredit a move of God by enticing God's people into compromising sexual situations. And so, it was in Thyatira. She taught and seduced God's servants to commit sexual immorality. This same spirit was rampant in the early days of the Holy Spirit's move among the gay community. It would take a radical awakening to bring about a shift in our thinking. AIDS was that wake-up call.

When I got to the airport, Rev. Troy also had a traveling companion from the L.A. headquarters with him. So, I took them both to their destination. Elder Troy was a perfect gentleman and he exuberantly reported on all the exciting things happening in the fellowship. It was inspiring. I also felt foolish for being so carnally minded, in those tight blue jeans, and swore I'd never do that again! I'd not inappropriately remove my underwear from then on! It was about then that I understood that God expected more of me and had a higher standard of conduct for me to abide by. I understood the message, I heard what God was saying, and chose to obey God. I'm glad I did.

The minister's conference was prophetic and uplifting. Afterward, I drove Rev. Elder Freda Smith and Elder John Hose with me to Grand Rapids for church and Freda was the one to preach. She preached a powerful message from Luke 9:62 on not looking back once you have decided to follow Jesus. She gave an example of a woman she knew who liked to water ski. But on one occasion the lake on which she skied had snakes along the water's edge. If she were to take her eyes off the boat and not look forward, she'd lose her balance and fall among the snakes. Freda said it was like that for us as Christians. We needed to fix our eyes on Jesus and not look back.

Once the service had ended and I took up an offering for these two Elders, I was embarrassed that the offering was only twenty-five dollars. I couldn't imagine giving these two powerful and anointed Elders a mere $12.50 apiece. But Rev. Freda was a true servant. She said it was an honor just to be in the church with us.

Months later, my pastor, Rev. Brenda Hunt, called me into her office. She handed me a brown paper bag. She said, "I guess this underwear is yours since they aren't mine."

Now I was really embarrassed. That was the end of me trying to catch someone's eye inappropriately. I never explained why my underwear was in her office, to begin with.

Rev. Troy Perry was not only instrumental in opening the doors of the inclusive gospel to the LGBT community but was also a catalyst for much social change. He was the main organizer of the first gay pride parade held in Los Angeles. He also fought for social and legal change for same-sex marriage.

On Sunday, March 14, 2004, Perry once wrote a poignant op-ed article in the **San Diego Union-Tribune** in favor of marriage before it was finally legalized. And it wouldn't be his last.

So MCC remains at the forefront of social action and the legislative fight for LGBT justice; as well as having the distinction of being the one place that opened the door to the gospel to those outside the camp. MCC has changed history, and one could never tell the stories of all the leaders she produced. There are great champions of the faith within the history of MCC, and there are many stories yet to be written.

Among the people who have left an indelible mark as the Holy Spirit used them to change the world in this particular flow of God was Jean White, a missionary to China and citizen of the United Kingdom who led MCC in world church extension. Also, Rev. Nancy Wilson was a champion of rights for LGBT people of faith and became the second MCC moderator after Rev. Perry retired. She is a prolific author whose books are worth reading to get a deeper insight into the theology of how God unfolded this mystery.[8]

Then also God used Delores Berry, a gospel singer, evangelist, and Spirit-filled woman of faith whose preaching, singing, and worship brought many LGBT people home to God. Marsha Stevens, a songwriter and evangelist whose most famous song, *For Those Tears I Died*, has led many of God's children to see that God loves them no matter where they have been.

Rev. Sky Anderson was a Trans-man whose journey and transition and testimony made many people see that the Trans community is totally included in God's heart and love. John Hose, John Gill, Ken Martin, Michael Mank, Arlene Ackerman, Paul Breton, Jack Isabell, Joan Wakeford, Renee McCoy, and so many others are among those God used to open the doors to the Gospel within the LGBT community.

They are hardly a comprehensive list of mighty saints God used. And I know I could never remember them all, but their stories and many others can be found at https://lgbtqreligiousarchives.org/profiles/

Yet, all in all, we still must take our hats off to Rev. Elder Troy D. Perry.

[1] http://mccchurch.org/overview/history-of-mcc/ last accessed October 16, 2015

[2] http://mccchurch.org/overview/history-of-mcc/ last accessed November 9, 2019

[3] http://www.mccchurch.org/ last accessed August 3, 2019

[4] http://www.amazon.com/The-Lord-Shepherd-Knows-Autobiography/dp/0938743007 (last accessed August 3, 2019

[5] http://www.amazon.com/Dont-Afraid-Anymore-Metropolitan-Community/dp/0312069545/ref=pd_sim_14_2?ie=UTF8&refRID=19AXKFJ90VGQND1N27EF&dpID=41PYRTrcsAL&dpSrc=sims&preST=_AC_UL160_SR160%2C160_ (last accessed October 16, 2015

[6] http://www.amazon.com/s/ref=nb_sb_ss_sc_1_17?url=search-alias%3Dstripbooks&field-keywords=rubyfruit+jungle&sprefix=ruby+fruit+jungle%2Cstripbooks%2C368 last accessed October 16, 2015

[7] Downs, Jim: *Stand By Me, The Forgotten History of Gay Liberation* Basic Books, NY, NY 2016 pg.63

[8] Wilson, Rev. Dr. Nancy, *Outing the Bible: Queer Folks, God, Jesus, and the Christian Scriptures,* 2013 and also:

Wilson, Rev. Dr. Nancy, *I Love to Tell the Story: 100+ Stories of Justice, Inclusion, and Hope,* 2016

The Early Travelling Evangelists

The Universal Fellowship of Metropolitan Community Churches had its own brand of traveling evangelists, and the Fellowship was not quite sure what to do with them. Since they were not pastoring churches, their ministerial credentials kept getting challenged. There were very few such evangelists in the beginning, and they were put through the ecclesiastical fire. But the anointing and the results could not be denied; many souls were coming to Christ. Eventually, the new Fellowship began to see the worth and value of these great pioneers and let them, and those to come later, bless the Body of Christ.

Ron Anderson

Rev. Ron Anderson had been a traveling evangelist in the days of the big tent revivals of the early 1960s. He had a wealth of experience and faith to add to this new movement. He had a huge bus and traveled the nation from one MCC church to another and wherever doors would open. Ron was not only a gifted musician and preacher but a true evangelist in the purest sense of the word. He had team members who traveled with him from city to city, though sometimes the team members would change, yet Rev. Anderson stayed the course. His messages were powerful demonstrations of the Word of God and I saw many LGBT people come to know Christ as their own Savior when the New Freedom Evangelistic Team pulled into town. I still pastored the MCC church in Grand Rapids, Michigan in 1981, when his enormous tour bus rolled into town.

We were forever indebted to his visit. Prior to his ordination with MCC, Pastor Ron had traveled a number of years with the great miracle worker A.A. Allen.

Rev. Ron told me his story over the years that I knew him:

Pastor Anderson shared that he entered the ministry with the Assembly of God denomination while attending the University of Nevada. During those years, he held tent revivals up and down the West Coast, held revivals at churches, and spent two years in Old Mexico building three churches and an orphanage that still exists today. Then he "left the Assemblies of God to do my own evangelistic work in the 'straight world'. Anderson shared that "during that time I was with AA Allen for a time. *Asa Alonso Allen, better known as A. A. Allen, was a minister with a Pentecostal evangelistic healing and deliverance ministry. He was, for a time, associated with the "Voice of Healing" movement founded by Gordon Lindsay. He died at the age of 59 in San Francisco, California. Allen was buried at his ministry headquarters in Miracle Valley, Arizona.*[1] Many miracles are documented through his ministry including the dead being raised. Since Anderson was closeted about his homosexuality and felt it was sinfully wrong, he was surprised to find other gay men on the trail with A.A. Allen. He found himself in a same-sex relationship with one team member, and due to the guilt he felt, he eventually left the team. He told me that on the bus were bunkbeds where he and his partner slept together with another couple above them. The morning after a night of a sexual encounter, they'd repent and ask God's forgiveness. Once he left A.A. Allen's ministry, he said: "I was booked for over a year to do revivals, when I gave God two weeks to change me (his sexual orientation) or I would leave the ministry. God didn't - and so I did; only to run into MCC in San Diego, California in the spring of 1969. The MCC fellowship was just getting started. I hated it and thought they were all going straight to hell in a "hand-basket". Two weeks later, a member of the church, Joseph Gilbert, talked me into going back to MCC to hear Rev. Troy Perry. My life would never be the same." Anderson continued: I became a member of MCC in

San Diego in 1969, became a deacon, exhorter (student clergy were called exhorters back then), and licensed in the spring of 1972. I then was the associate pastor with Rev. Elder Freda Smith, who was just plain reverend at that time. I was the deacon at the.

Sacramento MCC when she first attended. She then joined and became a clergy prior to my licensing. I was still fighting to go back into the ministry. Troy came up from LA and both of them "ganged up" on me to reenter the ministry. I then became the pastor of the MCC in Ft. Worth, TX. Then, I was ordained in 1976 at the General Conference in Washington D.C. at which time I started the New Freedom Evangelistic team shortly afterward. We went on the field that fall (1976) and held our first renewal at the Oklahoma City MCC. It caught on very quickly, and we were booked up for renewals a year in advance.

It was mostly lay people (congregations) that wanted us to hold a renewal at their church. We got very little support from the "leadership" of UFMCC or the churches. Our ministry was not officially recognized by UFMCC for a number of years. Therefore, at the request of the UFMCC, we became incorporated, obtained our own 501c3 status, and were an independent ministry. It was during the 2nd year that we had the hardest time staying on the field financially. We stopped in Salt Lake City, UT, and were very fortunate that one of our team members was a registered nurse. Jeanne Leggett went to work at the local hospitals (maternity wards) and put us back on the field just in time for the Denver, CO general conference.

From that point on, the team was a dynamic success in all areas and could not be ignored any longer by the "leadership". The team went from $1,400 in income and expenses in 1976 to over $40,000 in income and expenses in 1982. That was totally supplied by the local churches. Every team member received a $20 stipend per week, including myself. The total amount of the income went toward ministry except for those small stipends. The cost of staying at campgrounds went from $14 per night to over $47 per night in 1983. New Freedom Evangelistic Team was on the road, holding five-day renewals in different churches each week for 11 months out of the year for 7 1/2 years. There was a total of

18 people that served on the team; some of them for years and some for just 1 year or less.

The largest team was seven members at one time and the smallest was two during, 1 year. We started with a very old, converted school bus that we gutted and converted ourselves. It broke down 2 years later at which time we converted a new school bus. Then, in 1980 we converted a Silver Eagle bus (Continental Trailways) that put us up there with the "big guys" and the country western singers. We met many singing groups as we traveled in the United States and Canada. Clouds of Glory, Happy Goodman Family, Speer Family, Tammy &; Jim Bakker were just a few of those that we made friends with. In addition to traveling as an evangelist to the churches, within MCC, I started eight new churches and put many churches back on their feet. Our primary intent was to bring people to Jesus Christ.

We left the field when it became too expensive, and the extensive traveling had taken a toll on my health. At first, I was just taking a couple of years off, but God had other ideas and led me into pasturing." In 1991, Rev. Anderson became the pastor of Morning Star MCC, in Worcester, MA. His predecessor to that church, Rev. Emmett Watkins, had died of AIDS, and so upon accepting the pastorate he discovered a revival weekend had already been planned. I was the guest speaker. Ron didn't know me that well, so rather than cancel me, he added another speaker who he knew well, Rev. Bonnie Daniel. It turned out that weekend was her birthday and mine, both on the same day. Rev. Ron knew it was Bonnie's birthday, so he planned a surprise birthday party for her after the Sunday service.

That particular birthday was a pivotal one for me, and I did not want to celebrate it; I refused to acknowledge it to anyone. But here we were celebrating a birthday for Bonnie on my birthday, with cake, ice cream, and all the trimmings, so I secretly celebrated my birthday anyway. God made me laugh over that one. I tried to hide it, and God celebrated it anyway! The next day, on the way to the airport, my hosts asked, "by the way, when is your birthday?" When I gave them the date, they realized it was yesterday, and they felt horrible that Bonnie's was celebrated and mine was not. I assured them that mine was celebrated also, but secretly between me and God. I loved it! But for years after that my hosts (Michael Simpson and David Stebbins) sent me a birthday card.

Over the years, as Rev. Anderson pastored in Worchester, eventually, his church became an independent one, joining the Alliance of Christian Churches. Yes, we'll get to them later as well. In those traveling years Rev. Ron Anderson brought many people to Christ. Ron and his team were especially a huge blessing in remote areas where little churches had fewer resources to afford to bring people in to encourage their saints. I know our little church in Grand Rapids, Michigan was one such church blessed by their ministry. Rev. Anderson, Pastor of North Star Cathedral of Hope Church in Worcester, passed away unexpectedly Thursday, December 24th, 2015. Rev. Anderson touched many lives throughout a 50-year ministry His legacy lives on.

Jeri Ann Harvey

Jeri Ann Harvey was a well-known minister in the early days. She was Spirit-filled and spirited. She at one time pastored some of the largest MCC churches in the USA, including the mother church in Los Angeles and Houston. But then a shift happened, she left the pastorate, and she began to evangelize around the country. She had a huge impact as a result. I heard her speak on many occasions. It was always powerful and life changing.

Previous to the AIDS crisis, Jeri Ann Harvey once told how when she was pastoring the church in Houston, a gay guy she knew confessed that he had been in a Houston gay bathhouse for a weekend. He bragged about having 70 sexual partners that weekend. When she would tell that story we would all gasp in shock. That was really excessive by any standards! She said she wasn't sure whether she should congratulate him, pray for him, or just cry.

But cry we did, at funeral after funeral in those early days of AIDS. We thank God that Jeri Ann Harvey got good news into the hearts of many LGBT people who were on their way to destruction without it.

But during that time, she buried way too many friends — particularly from the HIV/AIDS epidemic.

Rev. Elder Jeri Ann Harvey was born January 3, 1934, in Oklahoma City, Oklahoma (USA) into a Cherokee nation family. This heritage was an important aspect of Jeri Ann's identity. She graduated from high school in 1952 and received her Bachelor of Science degree from the University of Oklahoma in 1961. She served two years with the United States Navy (1952-1954) and was honorably discharged. **Rev, Harvey** studied theology at Oklahoma Southwestern University. Prior to the ministry, Harvey had several articles and poetry published and was recorded as a singer with the Nelson Riddle Orchestra in 1953[2]

She traveled all over the world to reach one more sheep for the Good Shepherd. She gave until it hurt and loved as deeply, and it was felt. The stories of her life and ministry became unforgettable. She single-handedly confronted the Ku Klux Klan in Texas when they tried to intimidate her and threaten her church. She also defined the term "butch lesbian" for many! But Rev. Elder Jeri Ann was well-known in MCC as having a healing touch. She held healing services at MCC's General Conferences which were always well-attended. Her last General Conference was in Alberta, Calgary (Canada) in 2005 where her final healing service was packed with 500 people.[3] "You could feel the presence, the healing presence of Jesus and the power of the Holy Spirit. To be around her was to expect miracles, and to receive them. Even her presence was healing."[4]

One person wrote on her obituary page: Jeri-Ann Harvey brought me to the Lord. I went to MCC LA looking for a lover and instead I found Jesus. I will always be thankful to her for that.[5] Jeri Ann was living proof that God was moving in the midst of the LGBT community.

Finally, Jeri Ann moved to Spain with her spouse, Rev. Elder Gill Storey, and died at home on May 28, 2008.

[1] Biography Of A. A. Allen - Believers Portal (https://believersportal.com/biography-of-a-a-allen/) last accessed July 8, 2022.

[2] https://lgbtqreligiousarchives.org/profiles/jeri-ann-harvey (last accessed August 3, 2019)

[3] ibid

[4] https://rememberingjeriann.wordpress.com/2008/05/28/rev-elder-jeri-ann-harvey-2/ (last accessed August 3, 2019)

[5] https://vcattitudes.blogspot.com/2008/05/remembering-rev-jeri-ann-harvey.html (last accessed August 3, 2019)

Other Movers and Shakers

Freda Smith and Her Purple Grass

The Rev. Elder Freda Smith was the former Vice-Moderator of the Universal Fellowship of Metropolitan Community Churches; a political activist in California; and an advocate for women's and minority concerns. She was widely known for her tireless advocacy and concern for LGBT and minority rights. She has been recognized by the Sacramento History Museum as a "Woman of Courage," and was named "Woman of the Year" by the California State Legislature in 1996. Smith entered the Universal Fellowship of Metropolitan Community Churches in 1971. She first met the Reverend Elder Troy Perry on the steps of the Capitol of the State of California where they were both speakers for a rally to pass the "Consenting Adults Law," to decriminalize gay relationships in California. During a lobbying effort for the passage of the bill, Freda read her narrative poem, "Dear Dora/Dangerous Derek Diesel Dyke," to a select group of legislators which included Lt. Governor Merv Dymally. Dymally was visibly moved by the poem and stated that the poem had "opened his eyes." Later, Dymally historically broke the tie that had dead-locked the California Senate to pass California's Consenting Adults Law.

Freda was an early champion of women's concerns and was instrumental in spearheading the revision of UFMCC Bylaws to include women at every level of ministry. She was the first woman ordained to the UFMCC ministry and in 1973 was first elected to the Board of Elders. She was re-elected as an elder for five more terms during which time she served as World Church Extension Elder, liaison to Europe, Canada, Australia, and U.S. Districts, and as Vice-Moderator of the UFMCC. She appeared nationally on the Tomorrow Show in the U.S., on Canada AM, and on local broadcasts where she frequently debated right-wing religious political advocates.[1]

But even with all those accolades, her story is hardly told. Rev. Freda Smith was originally from Pocatello, a small town in Idaho in the USA. She was raised as a Nazarene. After WWII, she independently left to become a member of the Salvation Army. She had a fire in her bones for the gospel, God, and for social justice. Freda paved the pathway for women in ministry in MCC. She single-handedly changed the culture. But she also brought many to know this Good Shepherd who would go out of His way to find the lost sheep. The lost sheep that was lost because it wandered away, certain that it didn't fit in with the other sheep in the fold because, unlike the other sheep, it liked purple grass. Her sermon on Purple Grass changed the hearts of many towards God and brought healing to many who had been rejected by churches and families. It was recorded on cassette and played around the world; over and over and over again. Freda knew that Good Shepherd well. The little sheep that liked purple grass, was rejected from the flock because that little sheep was different. The flock went so far as to tell it that the Good Shepherd hated the little sheep. But the Good Shepherd searched high and low, then found it and personally brought the little lost sheep home. Yes, Jesus loves the outcasts. I've been told that her sermons can still be seen on YouTube.

Jesus personally and visibly touched Freda many times. One of her more memorable stories is how she was in a General Conference but in much pain. Her ankle was swollen. But during that worship service, God just reached down and healed her ankle without her even asking for it. Another proof of how God loves us.

For decades, Rev. Elder Freda Smith pastored the MCC in Sacramento, California. In 1985 the MCC International General Conference was held in her city. At that time, I pastored the MCC in Melbourne, Australia, and flew from there to attend the General Conference in Sacramento. It was the best of times and the worst of times for me. My spouse, Robert Shisler, was not with me in Australia. We could not get a visa for him to live with me in Melbourne, and my heart was breaking, missing him every day. Gay relationships were not legally recognized, and he did not have a career path that Australia accepted for him to be granted residency. They did not need another antique dealer. They granted visas to doctors or nurses or other professionals they needed. That wasn't Robert. So, he still lived in our home in Dayton, Ohio. Robert flew to Sacramento to be with me for this conference. While we were both in the States, we wanted to have a Holy Union; a wedding without the legal protections, since none were afforded us yet. It was the best a couple could do. We hoped we could get Freda to perform our wedding for us after the conference was over. But once the conference ended, Freda and her partner Kathleen, left for their retreat home in the mountains of California on the American River. We had no way of reaching her to even ask her. I would have to head back to Australia, broken-hearted once again, and Robert would have to go back to Ohio. But during the conference, while I was in the business meetings, Robert helped the local church folks in the background, making packets and handouts for the conference. Thus, he met some of Freda's local congregants. We asked them what the chance of would be getting a Holy Union before I left to return to Melbourne. This was a Divine appointment. They knew the secret code, to reach Freda and got her OK to bring us out to her retreat home. They whisked us in their car to this most beautiful location where we were greeted by a gentle and hospitable Elder and servant of God. Rev. Smith performed our Holy Union for us on a quaint little bridge on her property that straddled the American River. She made the day a memorable blessing. That is how she is: loving and gracious, generous, caring, and compassionate.

On December 3, 2019, we all heard the sad news that Elder Freda Smith had died. She had a stroke which led to pneumonia, and she passed away in the care of Hospice. She was survived by her long-term spouse Kathleen. Rev. Troy Perry posted a memorial to her on his Facebook page. It read:

MCC Mourns the Passing of Rev. Elder Freda Smith

22 November 1935-3 December 2019

Rev. Elder Freda Smith has inspired a generation of women, lesbians, and people of every gender and orientation. Just yesterday, we learned that Freda was placed into hospice care, and today we heard that she died. We give thanks for the compassionate care of hospice, and we pray for her long-time spouse of 40 years, Kathleen Meadows.

There aren't many people in the history of the movement of Metropolitan Community Churches that have been as instrumental as Rev. Elder Freda Smith. And we pause together to give thanks and to honor her life and her contribution. Not only did she inspire and change MCC, but she also worked tirelessly and courageously in her state of California for legislative change as an early political activist.

Freda came from a Nazarene and Salvation Army background, and she was the first woman ordained in MCC, as well as the first woman elected as an Elder. In fact, for all who remember her, her story is THE story that will always be told about MCC in terms of inclusive language. At one of our early General Conferences, Freda noticed that most of the terms for pastors or leaders were exclusively male; so, Freda asked for all the bylaws to be changed so that "he" could become "he or she," or something more inclusive. (She was ahead of her time in asking for a quick "search and replace.") Freda was told our process did not allow for that kind of change. Nevertheless, she persisted. Freda stood up EVERY TIME there was a gender-specific word in MCC bylaws and petitioned for it to be changed to "he or she" instead of only "he." Rev. Elder Freda Smith is the one we should credit for bringing about inclusive language as an early value and guiding principle of MCC.

Two other contributions of note include:

1. Freda wrote a poem called "Dear Dora" that was read in the California Legislature in the early 1970s, and in countless other churches in these last 40 years.

2. Freda was the one who gave a sermon entitled, "Purple Grass," which is now the name of an MCC award that honors those who have exceptional gifts in evangelism and preaching.

Rev. Elder Troy Perry, the Founder of Metropolitan Community Churches reminds us, "Freda Smith was a member of the Board of Elders and the Vice Moderator of our denomination. As most of us know, she was also the first woman ordained in MCC. Freda has shaped this movement as much as anyone has, and we have lost a hero."

Rev. Elder Don Eastman, former Vice Moderator for MCC, says:

"Rev. Elder Freda Smith was a true apostle of Jesus Christ in our lives and world. With the heart of a pastor and the voice of a prophet, she was a passionate and eloquent herald of the inclusive gospel -- good news -- that God gave Rev. Troy Perry and Metropolitan Community Churches. She was a formidable advocate for justice and inclusion. As an evangelist, Freda was a powerful witness of God's unconditional love and acceptance for all people. She brought that message to many thousands of people in our churches and communities.

In her ministry as an Elder, Freda was often a pastor to pastors. She inspired, challenged, enlightened, and encouraged us. Like the apostle Paul was to the Corinthians, to many of us Freda was a spiritual parent. By her word and example, she nurtured our growth as servant leaders.

Rev. Freda Smith's influence will continue in the days and years ahead. The inspiration of her faithful life and ministry abides to encourage us as we carry on MCC's mission to transform ourselves as we transform the world."

On her website, Freda said this was her final prayer, as an evangelist: "When I stand before God at the end of my life, I would hope that I would not have a single bit of talent left and that I could say, 'I used everything you gave me.'" We are confident this is the absolute truth about Freda, and that we have been the grateful recipients of so many of her gifts.

Yes, Freda is one grand lady, a class act, and a powerful saint of Almighty God. We will rejoice when we see her once again in Heaven; but in the meantime, her legacy is rich and lives on. Certainly, Rev. Elder Freda Smith will be forever stamped in my heart as a saint who touched lives, one soul or one church or one denomination or one nation at a time.

[1] http://www.lgbtran.org/Profile.aspx?ID=18 last accessed October 17, 2015

The Early Pentecostals and William Carey

For quite a time, MCC was the only affirming church available for LGBT folks to be safe and loved and accepted as they were. Because Rev. Troy Perry himself came from a Pentecostal background, there were some local churches that had a Pentecostal flavor to them. But the vast majority of MCC churches were more liturgical in nature. Generally speaking, it depended on the preference of the Senior Pastor, especially if they were the founder. One example of that was Rev. Lin Stoner who began Redeemer MCC in Flint Michigan in 1980. She was from a Pentecostal holiness background, and for all the years that she pastored, she kept her "crown of glory", her long Pentecostal hairdo rolled up into a beehive. Her services were always Christ-centered and Spirit-filled. The same thing was true of Reconciliation MCC of Grand Rapids, MI, when she became the pastor there.

Left to right is Rev. Jim Lynch on the far left. Rev. Lin Stoner in front.
I am on the far right, Rev. Dan Bennett, another MCC minister, in
the back; at Reconciliation MCC Grand Rapids' 25th Anniversary.

Rev. Lin was a well-beloved, Holy Spirit POWERHOUSE. She brought many people to Christ and many lives were changed under her ministry. Since she ministered both in Flint and then Grand Rapids, she really changed the spiritual landscape in Michigan. However, unless they could meet up with her, her lone church in either Flint or Grand Rapids, could not possibly meet the needs of the majority of other Pentecostal believers throughout the entire nation. It was inevitable that those from a Pentecostal background would want more than the liturgical Episcopalian style service generally offered within MCC.

Additionally, within the world of Pentecostal churches, there was a division between Oneness and Trinitarian believers that dated back to the early 1900s.

Oneness Pentecostalism (also known as Apostolic, Jesus' Name Pentecostalism, or the Jesus Only movement) is a nontrinitarian religious movement within Protestant Pentecostalism. Its distinction from other

Pentecostal Christianity is its teaching on the Godhead, referred to as the Oneness doctrine which states that there is one God, a singular divine spirit with no distinction of persons who manifests himself in many ways, including as Father, Son, and Holy Spirit. Trinitarian theology believes in three distinct and eternal persons separate but equal as manifested by the Father, Son, and Holy Spirit.

Additionally, Oneness believers baptize believers in the name of Jesus Christ alone as opposed to the Trinitarian formula of baptizing "in the name of the Father, the Son, and the Holy Spirit." Oneness believers affirm that Jesus is the one and only name of the Father, Son, and Holy Spirit. As a result, these doctrinal beliefs differed even within the LGBT Christian community, and it was soon felt that something other than MCC was needed to accommodate these Christians.

The movement to create LGBT-affirming Apostolic or Oneness Pentecostal churches began on July 28, 1980, when Reverend William H. Carey started the National Gay Pentecostal Alliance (NGPA). The organization opened its first church in Omaha, Nebraska in 1981. Thus, Reverend William H. Carey was the founder of the affirming Apostolic Pentecostal movement. He envisioned an international network of affirming Oneness Pentecostal churches, including the more fundamentalist theology inherent with such churches. The first three ministers were Rev. William Carey, E. Samuel Stafford, and Frances Cervantes. Later in 1983, the Reverend Sandy Lewis, District Elder, and Reverend Phildora Prigmore came into the NGPA organization in Tucson, Az to further the movement.[1]

Although NGPA was an Apostolic (Oneness) Pentecostal organization, due to the lack of affirming Trinitarian Pentecostal churches, NGPA originally welcomed all affirming Pentecostals into fellowship. Eventually Trinitarian Pentecostals began to organize their own churches and organizations at which point NGPA became fully Oneness Pentecostal.

Rev. Carey reported that over the next decade, NGPA included congregations in California, Arizona, Massachusetts, Alabama, New York, Georgia... as well as other places. We also helped support a mission in Cross River State, Nigeria. Later, we had a mission in Donetsk Oblast, Ukraine, and contacts in St. Petersburg, Russia.

Rev. William Carey: founder of the National Gay Pentecostal
Alliance. (NGPA) then and now.

Rev. Carey moved to Schenectady, New York in 1984 and opened Lighthouse Apostolic Church, and was pastor there until 1997. NGPA changed its name to Apostolic Restoration Mission (ARM) and changed the name of its Bible School (founded in 1981 as Pentecostal Bible Institute) to Apostolic Institute of Ministry (AIM). ARM later merged with GAAAP (Global Alliance of Affirming Apostolic Pentecostals), under the GAAAP name.

GAAAP was organized in 2007 by Rev. Kevin Konkle then of Indianapolis, Indiana, and Rev. Robert Morgan of Tampa, Florida. Rev. Robert Morgan served as Founding Chairman and Rev. Konkle as Founding Vice-Chairman. Rev. Robert Morgan had been a leader within another Pentecostal organization: Reconciling Pentecostals International (RPI). But in 2003 he and the other leaders had a split over theological concerns which surfaced at their conference held at Rev. Morgan's church in Tampa, Fl.

(More on this later)

GAAAP originally began as a ministerial fellowship, growing from only 2 founding ministers at the beginning of 2007 to 17 ministers by early 2008. By late fall 2010, the organization had grown to over 60 ministers in 19 States and 5 nations, In April 2010, GAAAP assumed the 501c3 offered by the Apostolic Restoration Mission (ARM), formerly known as the National Gay Pentecostal Alliance (NGPA). NGPA had been the first LGBT-affirming Apostolic denomination, having been formed in 1980 by Rev. William Carey. A schism within this organization in 2010 reduced those numbers.

Ultimately, GAAAP was turned over to Rev. Joseph Parramore who brought the organization under his leadership and ministry where it remains today as New Journey Fellowship in Florida.[2]

[1]   https://en.m.wikipedia.org/wiki/Global_Alliance_of_Affirming_Apostolic_Pentecostals last accessed August 8, 2022

[2] ibid

Community Gospel Church, Houston and Fellowship

While I was at that MCC General Conference in Sacramento California, I met this very tall, very engaging black man named Emmett Watkins. It turns out he was the pastor of the MCC in Worchester, Massachusetts and he was also a prophet who happened to have AIDS. Out of nowhere, Emmet walked over to me during a conference break and began to prophesy over me. I was quite surprised. Then he told me God had made a connection between us in the Spirit. At first, I blew it off not sure what to make of this guy. But he was serious. Later that year, after pastoring the MCC in Melbourne, Australia, I came back home to Ohio to live with my spouse Robert. I wasn't sure what God had for me next since I wasn't willing to again leave Robert in order to pastor a church the way I did to go to Australia. But I had no real options in Dayton. I had already been the pastor of that MCC, and they had a new pastor and had moved on.

Perhaps, I thought, I would do like Jeri Ann Harvey, and be an evangelist. At the time MCC had 250 churches in the USA and I wrote to all of them. I introduced myself and sent a resume stating I would be available for a weekend revival if desired. The church I founded in Grand Rapids, Michigan requested me to come for a weekend, and so did a church I had visited frequently in Flint, Michigan. Once those two weekends were accomplished nothing else happened. It seemed I wasted 248 stamps. I got a response from the MCC in Quincy, Illinois which basically said, "Who are you, again?" So that went nowhere. Then as I fasted and waited on the Lord, in April of 1986 an independent LGBT

Pentecostal church in Houston called me and asked if I'd come for a revival. I never heard of Community Gospel Church before. But they were "the Pentecostal family of Montrose" (the predominately gay neighborhood of Houston, Texas). Community Gospel Church in Houston began in 1981.

Pastor Ronnie Pigg pastored his first church in southeastern Oklahoma before moving to Oklahoma City where he served as a youth pastor. At the age of 21, he recognized his inner struggle and decided to leave the church and come out as an openly gay man. Then at age 23 he decided to go back to the church and began serving as a worship leader, youth pastor, and assistant pastor within the Pentecostal Holiness denomination. After being ordained about a year later, someone called and "outed" him to this denomination and he was abruptly dis-fellowshipped and stripped of his credentials.

Not easily shaken in mind or deed, Pastor Ronnie began to pray for direction and guidance and heard about a group of Pentecostal gays and lesbians in Houston that had started under the leadership of the late Rev. Alvis Strickland, the Community Gospel Church. Pastor Ronnie was asked by this group to be a guest speaker for one service at a revival meeting they were conducting. While there he felt direction from the Lord to relocate to Houston. After a brief period, the pastor resigned, and Pastor Ronnie was asked to fill the pulpit and served there from 1985-1992. During his tenure there, Pastor Ronnie started a network of affirming Pentecostal churches that were known as Community Gospel Fellowship.[1] But Rev. Ronnie Pigg was the fourth person to pastor Community Gospel Church in Houston.

The founder, Alvis Strickland began the work. According to the NGPA founder, William Carey, Alvis Strickland traveled to Omaha, where they were having the first General Conference of the NGPA (1982). Thus, Community Gospel Church of Houston became part of NGPA, and four people from the Omaha church, including Carey, moved to Houston. CGC was a large congregation and Alvis Strickland was a dynamic preacher.

But, according to Rev. William Carey, he was also a problem. He didn't believe in the existence of Satan and was neither Trinitarian nor

Oneness. But the worst part of this was that *he never explained what he believed* but persisted in ridiculing both Trinity and Oneness folks from the pulpit. Around this time, another Community Gospel Church opened in Dallas and joined NGPA. But as Presbyter, Rev. Carey had to speak to pastor Strickland in Houston about verbally/spiritually abusing the saints. Strickland took offense and pulled the church out of NGPA. Additionally, he also owned the house where the Dallas pastor lived and threatened to evict him if he didn't pull Dallas out of NGPA. NGPA opened a new congregation in Houston, which Carey believed was called the Church of Pentecostal Unity, with Billy O. Brown as pastor. From that point forward, NGPA was strictly Oneness. Future CGC churches were Trinitarian, so there was no longer a need for them to be part of NGPA.[2]

Strickland also had an associate pastor, a brother named David Bronson. For some reason Alvis and David had a disagreement and Alvis abruptly left town without a word and that left Brother Bronson as their second pastor.

But David Bronson was HIV (+) and did not know that the droppings from his pet birds could be deadly. He quickly passed away and next came two people to fill the pulpit. They were Rev. (Era) Lois O'Neal and Rev. Chris Wellington. It became difficult to keep the two pastors flowing in unity, so Rev. Chris Wellington graciously stepped down, and Rev. O'Neal became the next pastor.

Lois stayed in the pulpit for several months, and then one day she came to church with a bowl of water and washed her hands in front of the church. As she did so she declared that she washed her hands of all of them and resigned. Rev. Ronnie Pigg became the next pastor and was there for several years. He was pastoring when I was asked to come to Houston for a revival in 1986. Following Rev. Ronnie Pigg, once Ronnie resigned, the church had Rev. Chris Wellington become the pastor. He led it for many faithful years. Occasionally, Lois still fellowshipped with the church, and when I first came to preach there in April 1986, she was present. I met her and knew she was one special woman.

When our church in Dayton began, I often had Lois come to preach a revival for us. She would preach with old-timey Holy Ghost fire, yes, but she was also anointed as a musician and singer. She played guitar and was a one-woman revival! Sometime after she left Community Gospel Church, she started another Pentecostal church of about 40 people also in Houston. This was a great blessing, but Louis was more of an evangelist and was happiest when she preached revivals. We were especially blessed when she came to Dayton to hold a revival for us in July 1992.

Finally, on November 13, 2019, I got the news that Lois O'Neal had passed away from complications after surgery.

I remember that for many years Lois had back problems, and she once told me a story about going to see a back surgeon in Houston named Dr. Goldstein. The doctor had her on a radiology table to do a procedure on her back to help with her back pain. The procedure was painful and to keep her mind off the pain, she kept saying: "Oh, Thank you, Jesus!"

Dr. Goldstein was put off by all this praise to the Christian God, and told her: "Listen, lady, if I was you, I'd be saying 'Thank you, Goldstein'. I'm the one helping you here!"

So, without missing a beat, Lois began saying, "Oh thank you, Goldstein, thank you, Jesus, thank you, Goldstein, Thank you, Jesus!" She was quite sincere.

Rev. Lois O'Neal

Michael Bush, a longtime friend wrote of Lois:

> I got word yesterday from Pastor Ronnie and Pastor Samuel about the passing of our dear Sister Lois. Ever since then my emotions have run the gamut of smiles and tears. I guess we just clicked the first time we met, and over the years we have shared a lot of smiles and tears. I'll never forget the time she taught her church about looking at appearances. Church time was approaching, and Lois still hadn't shown up and folks were getting worried. Right about time

for church the back door opened, and a bag lady walked in. She had dirty clothes, a face and hair that didn't look like they had seen soap and water in a long time, and a smell that wasn't much better. The look on the faces of the congregation ran the gamut from 'poor thing' to backing over to other chairs hoping she wouldn't sit by them. She wandered around for a few minutes, looking at the faces of those that were shunning her. A few more minutes, she walked toward the pulpit, dropped the dirty coat she had on, pulled off the wig and the dirty clothes, and there stood Lois. She looked at the congregation and said something to the effect of I think you all need to repent. As well as I remember she never preached a sermon...she didn't need to!

My partner Mark passed away in 1996. His funeral was on a Saturday, and I didn't even try to go to church on Sunday. I got a call from Lois on Monday...how you are doing, etc. We chatted for a few minutes, and she asked me if I had gone to church, and I said I just couldn't handle it. She asked if I felt like having company over the coming weekend, guess I said OKAY cause she said Rose and I will be there on Saturday to go to church with me. I tried to tell her she didn't need to do that...did you ever try to talk Lois out of something? She cinched it when she asked me if I was going the next Sunday and I said I just don't think I could. Needless to say, she and Rose arrived Saturday, and we laughed and cried and did it some more. Sunday morning arrives and my mind is working trying to figure out how to get out of this. Lois took me by the shoulders and said, "little brother we can do this." We get to church, and I wanted to sit at the back, she looked at me and asked where Mark and I sat. I walked to the second row and said Mark set in the second seat, and I was on the aisle. One of them set in the 3rd seat, me in the 2nd, and the other on the aisle. Between them holding my hands and holding me while I cried, I made it thanks to Lois and Rose. I'm sorry this is so long, but I wanted to share my thoughts about my friend and big sister, Reverend Era Lois O'Neal. Until we meet again... God speed my friend.

Between 1981and 1982 at least three independent, non-MCC churches sprung up in the gay community. Grace Gospel Church in Seattle, which was an LGBT evangelical church; Faith Temple which was an LGBT Pentecostal church within the black community of Washington D.C., and Community Gospel Church in Houston. Also in its beginning stages was the first of seven Christ Chapel churches begun as a bible study in the home of Michael Cole in Long Beach, California.

Since Robert, my spouse, was an antique dealer, he often set up at various antique shows around the nation and knew many other dealers. We had a friend, another antique dealer named Dick Weaver. He occasionally traveled with Robert. He once lived in Ohio but had since moved to Houston, Texas, and was attending Community Gospel Church. In April 1986, Rev. Ronnie Pigg, though not the founder, was the current pastor of the church. Since there were no other churches like theirs anywhere that they knew of, and they wanted to hold a revival, they were asking around if anyone knew any preachers available. Dick knew Robert and knew that I was a preacher recently returned from Australia. He suggested me.

Pastor Ronnie asked if Dick had ever heard me preach. He said, "No, but I know how they live their life." That was good enough for him, so I was asked if I'd come for a revival weekend. Robert knew of an antique and flea market in Canton, Texas that we could go to the weekend before, which would finance our trip to Houston. So, it was settled. That revival was powerful, and God moved on many hearts. Several people got baptized that weekend: both in water and also in the Holy Spirit. And the weekend revival kept on going for the whole week.

Community Gospel Church of Houston. The Pentecostal Family of Montrose.
Rev. Ronnie Pigg is in the suit on the last row.

Rev. Ronnie Pigg preaching

Two elderly ladies who lived within walking distance, named Miss Grace and Miss Mary, attended the church because they liked it. They had no idea that they were the only heterosexuals in attendance. Ronnie Pigg had a spouse named DL Salisbury, who was also the worship leader. He was up on the platform with Pastor Ronnie. It was no secret that they were a couple; everyone knew it. Everyone, that is except Miss Mary and Miss Grace.

During one of the services, Mary turned to Grace and asked if she knew that there were homosexuals going to the church. Grace was shocked and said "No! Who?" Miss Mary pointed out a lesbian couple sitting in the front row. Miss Grace was astounded and asked Mary, "Does Pastor Ronnie know?" Now although these two elderly ladies were the only heterosexuals at Community Gospel, Miss Mary deduced that the butch women were lesbians and thus the only gay people in the sanctuary. Ha!

Christopher and Jonathan Wellington were actively engaged members of this Houston church. Chris was a talented musician, singer, evangelist, and preacher. He began a traveling evangelistic group called Revival. He held revivals around the nation with two other team members. DL Salisbury, Rev. Ronnie's husband, would be a part of this group, as well as Roseanne Lawrence.

Pastors Chris Wellington (left) and Jonathan Wellington (right). They Pastored Community Gospel in Houston after Rev. Ronnie Pigg left.

During that initial weeklong revival, the Holy Spirit clearly spoke to me that I needed to get ordained with this group. That meant one thing. At that time in MCC it was not possible to hold dual credentials. So, if I obeyed the Holy Spirit and got ordained with Community Gospel Church in Houston, I had to turn in my clergy credentials with MCC. I was not willing to argue with God, so I asked if they would ordain me. Pastor Ronnie said he hadn't been ordained by his church either, so in a dual ceremony, we both became ordained in Community Gospel Church. But what did that now mean? Was I to move to Houston? I knew Robert wouldn't leave Ohio. So, we traveled back home, and I sent my resignation to MCC without knowing what God wanted me to do with this new ordination out of Houston. I fasted, I waited, I prayed. Then the Lord spoke to me to start a Pentecostal church in the LGBT community in Dayton, Ohio: a second Community Gospel Church. I determined that I would not steal sheep from another church; if God wanted the second church in Dayton, God would have to bring in the people. I made a point of going to see the pastor of the MCC in Dayton to let her know that I was starting a new church, but that I would not invite any of her people, except her.

Through a Divine appointment, God gave me a co-pastor, Bill Roberts, who was formerly an Assemblies of God pastor. I had never pastored a Pentecostal church and wasn't sure what one would look like. I did know Bill Roberts had been a Pentecostal pastor, and since that was what God was asking of me, I knew I'd need his help. But he went to another church, and I refused to steal sheep from any other church. So, I prayed and fasted. At that time, I worked as a nurse during the 3-11 pm shift. While I was at work, Bill Roberts, who lived a few blocks away, decided to go jogging that night at about 10 pm. He jogged past our house. I did not know where he lived, and he did not know where we lived. But at the moment he was passing our house, the Holy Spirit demanded that he stop jogging and go knock on our door. That seemed weird because he didn't know who lived there. He obeyed and my spouse Robert answered the door and almost fell over! He told Bill that I had been praying for him to come by because I was starting a new church and wanted him to be a part of it. He further told Bill, to come in, have some cake (with Bill, it was always chocolate!), and that I'd be home from work soon. When I came home and saw Bill Roberts, the very man I'd been asking God to send by, sitting at our kitchen table eating chocolate cake, I knew God did this! I told Bill my plan to begin a Community Gospel Church as a Pentecostal church in Dayton, Ohio. He agreed to pray about it for three days and see what God said. At the time he was attending the MCC in Dayton that I had formerly pastored, but he was unappreciated. His gifts were not utilized very often, and so, at the end of three days, he told the pastor, Rev. La Paula Turner, that he was resigning. Then Bill let me know his answer was yes. He could play piano; he could lead worship. I had none of those abilities. In addition, he could powerfully preach. This was going to be great!

Samuel Kader, author, preaching at Community Gospel Church in Dayton

We set the date to begin on July 6, 1986. We rented space from the Unitarian Church, though they were reluctant to rent to us; not because we were gay, but because we were Pentecostal. Because in MCC we always had bulletins, I decided Bill and I needed to get together to plan the bulletin. He said we don't need bulletins.

I asked, "We don't? Then how will we know in what order things will happen in the service?"

Bill replied that the Holy Spirit would lead us.

I was dumbfounded. "He will?" Well, yes, He did, and we never had bulletins.

Soon after our church was up and running, there were now two Community Gospel Churches, so we formed a network called Community Gospel Fellowship. Within that year, other groups wanted to become Community Gospel Churches as well. There was one in California, one in Florida, and one in New Orleans. Soon there were six Community Gospel Churches.

Simultaneously as Community Gospel Churches were starting up, God had another group of Pentecostal churches being raised up, Grace Fellowship. They had their main church in Dallas, and another in New Orleans. And another independent Pentecostal church, Circle of Glory, also began in Ft. Worth, Texas. Its pastor was Thomas Henry Hirsch. In 1986, the church in Houston decided we needed to have a fellowship conference for minimally the Community Gospel Churches. As we planned it, the Grace Fellowship Churches joined us as did Circle of Glory in Ft. Worth. Rev. Thomas Hirsch asked if we would ordain him, and we agreed. So did the other four pastors of the churches within Community Gospel Fellowship. Grace Fellowship and Community Gospel pondered whether we should merge, but Grace Fellowship ultimately decided against it. After a short time, Grace Fellowship started their conference called SpiritFest. Six months later in 1987, Rev. Thomas Hirsch began yet another conference named Advance. And since he was nearby in Fort Worth, Rev. Ronnie Pigg of Houston attended.

He called me and said, "You have got to get down here for this!" I went to the next conference held yet another six months later, and we decided to join Advance as an organizational conference rather than have a separate one for Community Gospel Fellowship.

In 1982 there were only three independent churches in the LGBT community; but by 1986 when we began our church in Dayton, Ohio, independent churches were springing up everywhere. Advance became a national conference. Soon after, regional conferences that Rev. Hirsch called ACTS weekends also were birthed.

Sometime in 1986, I got a call from Rev. Emmett Watkins. He was that tall engaging black pastor in Worchester MA that I met in 1985 at the MCC General Conference. He wanted me to come to hold a revival. I explained that I was no longer in MCC, so I didn't know if that changed anything. He still wanted me to come, so I agreed. When I got there, I discovered Emmett had full-blown AIDS. He daily took a handful of experimental antiviral drugs for his HIV, but they left him exhausted. He had to sleep most of the day. I stayed in his home and tried to be quiet and study to let him get his rest. But when it came time for service, Emmett was an energized fireball. I saw how he meant we were connected in the Spirit as he had prophesied before. We flowed in the Spirit well together. The revival went well, and we were all blessed by the presence of the Lord. Emmett asked if I'd come back again. Of course, I agreed.

When I returned, in 1987, Emmett surprised me. MCC had yet another apostolic Elder who was a Charismatic leader, a mover, and a shaker who had impacted and founded churches all over the world. This was the Rev. Elder Lee Carlton. We both were guests at Emmett's home, and Emmett invited us both to preach at his church. On the first night of revival, Pastor Emmett announced that on the second night Rev. Lee Carlton and I were going to tag team preach; meaning we would be both preaching the sermon together alternating between us as the Spirit led. I was in a panic! What was THIS? I never heard of such a thing. So, the next afternoon while Rev. Watkins was sleeping, I asked Rev. Elder Carlton if he wanted to discuss what we would be doing so we could kind of get a handle on this. No, he didn't; that made me even more nervous! I guess I'd have to trust God to make this happen. I fasted, I studied, I poured over the Word of God. Then that evening, when it was time to preach, I started. But I soon ran out of things to say. Then Rev. Lee jumped right in and flowed into the stream. He stopped, and suddenly I knew what needed to be added. Once I stopped, He jumped in again. It went on like this until an entire outpouring of the Spirit's words had been delivered. I was particularly impressed with Rev. Elder Lee Carlton because he simply stayed in touch with God and flowed with wherever the Spirit was moving. I was amazed!

Rev. Carlton had many years of experience with the Holy Spirit and was truly an early pioneer in this move of God. His many years of ordained Christian ministry, beginning in April 1971 with MCC in Tampa, FL changed the spiritual landscape for LGBT people. Rev. Carlton had started many other churches and had additionally pastored the mother church in Los Angeles from 1972-1975. In 1975, he had been the founding pastor of MCC in Sydney, Australia. So, when I was in Melbourne ten years later, in 1985, I could get advice from him as an Elder in the fellowship. During his tenure, some 27 congregations of MCC were established in the US and abroad. Lee, himself traveled to and confirmed new works in Australia, New Zealand, Nigeria in Africa, England, Scotland, France, and Denmark in Europe. He welcomed new pastors, confirmed new church groups, and met with other interested groups. He ministered from Argentina to Australia, the Philippines to Sweden, and Africa to India. It was THIS minister of the gospel with whom Rev. Emmett had me tag team preach. I was not disappointed! It was an honor to spend a weekend with him.

Rev. Dusty Pruitt

In the fall of 1988, Rev. Emmett Watkins had me return for yet another revival. This time I was pleased to meet Rev. Sandra Turnbull, her spouse, Janet Robertson, and two other women who were traveling with them: Ronnie and Teri. The four of them were on an evangelistic crusade with the intent of traveling to every MCC church that would have them in to sing and bring the Gospel. They were sponsored by their home church, MCC Long Beach, California where Rev. Dr. Dusty Pruitt was their pastor. Thus, they had a legitimate spiritual covering and could use this as a recommendation to approach churches for a ministry opportunity. They were highly anointed, and I was impressed. Their goal was to reach every MCC that would open their doors, but I had an independent Pentecostal church in Dayton, Ohio: Community Gospel. So, I didn't know if they'd object to coming to a non-MCC church or not. They were delighted. Their tour was to last a year, so in early December they pulled up to our church in Ohio and ministered in the most powerful way. A strong spiritual bond was formed. Once their yearlong tour ended, they started their first Ministry Training School the following summer, in July 1990. I was honored to be the first MTS speaker, held at MCC Long Beach under the pastoral leadership of Dr. Dusty Pruitt. The intense training of the school lasted a week.

Rev. Tom Bigelow

Tom Bigelow pastored at MCC in Atlanta, and, while there, was instrumental in Ken Coulter's life. Ken went on to New Orleans to become the founder of the Grace Fellowship network of churches. Rev. Bigelow pastored among the MCC Churches in those early days and preached about the Baptism of the Holy Spirit. One such church was the MCC in Ft. Myers Florida, as well as others. Eventually Rev. Tom Bigelow left MCC altogether and became a priest in the Episcopalian church. The Episcopal Church was one of the streams that flowed in the Charismatic renewal in the 1960s spearheaded by Rev. Dennis Bennett [3].

According to an article in the King County Journal [4] dated May 21, 2003, Father Tom Bigelow came out as a gay man to his Episcopal congregation, St. Luke's in Renton, WA five years earlier. That announcement in 1998 completely changed the church. But though about a third of St. Luke's members left, Rev. Tom stayed on until his retirement. One direct result of that announcement by Rev. Bigelow was that a local PFLAG [Parents and Friends of Lesbians and Gays] chapter started.

In the early days of the Spirit-filled Gay Christian movement, it was common to find someone whose spiritual life had been impacted by Rev. Bigelow's ministry. Among them was my husband, Gerald Wright. After we became a couple in 2005, Jerry and I made a trip to Washington State and looked up Rev. Bigelow. He was still at St. Luke's in Renton, WA, though now retired, but still engaged in ministry and in the flow of the Holy Spirit. It was a lovely visit and a powerful night of ministry.

[1] http://www.lgbtran.org/Profile.aspx?ID=180 last accessed October 17, 2015

[2] From an online conversation with Rev. William Carey on August 8, 2022

[3] **Dennis J. Bennett** (October 28, 1917 - November 1, 1991) was an American Episcopal priest, who, in 1960, received the Baptism of the Holy Spirit. He was the Author of the seminal book *Nine O'Clock in the Morning* ISBN 0-88270-629-2. (https://en.wikipedia.org/wiki/Dennis_Bennett_%28priest%29) last accessed December 23, 2019

[4] [www.kingcountyjournal.com/sited/story/html/131969]

Gay Pentecostals and Evangelicals

Dr. James Tinney

The founder of Faith Temple, Rev. James Tinney, was a Professor at Howard University. Dr. James S. Tinney was a leading authority on the history of the Black press and on Black Pentecostalism. When he identified himself publicly as a gay man and founded a church for Black lesbians and gays, he was excommunicated from the Temple Church of God in Christ. Yet he persevered in his work as a journalism professor at Howard University and his ministry at Faith Temple in Washington, D.C.

Dr. James Tinney [1]

Tinney was born in Kansas City, Missouri. He exhibited an early and fervent interest in religion. He preached a three-week-long revival service at age 14 and became an ordained minister at age 18. During the 1960s, he was pastor of several churches in Arkansas and Missouri and was also an assistant editor of the *Kansas City Call*.

In 1962, he married Darlene Wood, and they had two daughters. The marriage ended in divorce in 1969 when Tinney came out to his wife, revealing his homosexuality. Immediately his wife and pastor rejected him and cut him off from family, children, and church.

Tinney lived quietly with two successive lovers who were also active Pentecostals.

In 1973, Tinney moved to Washington, D.C., and completed his graduate education in journalism at Howard University. During this period, he was the editor of *The Washington Afro-American* newspaper and a speechwriter for Rep. John Conyers (Michigan) and Samuel C. Jackson, undersecretary of the Department of Housing and Urban Development in the Nixon Administration.

In 1976, Tinney became an assistant professor of journalism at Howard University. He helped to establish the first scholarly journal on Black Pentecostalism, *Spirit: A Journal of Issues Incident in Black Pentecostalism*, as well as the William J. Seymour Pentecostal Fellowship at Howard, an annual Black Religion Writers Workshop, and the Society for Blacks in Religious Communications.

In 1979, Tinney came out publicly in an address to the initial Third World Lesbian and Gay Conference. In 1980, he founded the Pentecostal Coalition for Human Rights as part of his mission to help lesbians and gay men to reconcile their Pentecostalism with their homosexuality. In 1982, he organized a three-day revival for gays and lesbians. This resulted in Bishop Samuel Kelsey, the pastor of the church where Tinney served as a lay minister, excommunicating him. Later that year, on the third Sunday in September, Tinney founded Faith Temple, a nondenominational church with a largely Black gay and lesbian congregation. Through Faith Temple, Tinney organized several conferences to help build bridges between fundamentalist churches and the LGBT community. In 1987 Dr. Tinney had Elder's training and set apart Isaiah Poole, Michael Vanzant, Myaka Martin and another woman named Camille. Myaka and Camille both died in the 1990s.

1987 would have been the 5th anniversary of Faith Temple. I preached there for that anniversary and stayed in Tinney's DC home. His home was right in the heart of Washington and was a shotgun-style home. While there, I sat in the next room while Tinney counseled a young black man. The man was distraught because he was so promiscuous and didn't seem to be able to stop having indiscriminate sexual encounters. To my shock, Tinney told him that was nothing to be ashamed of; that these continuous sexual encounters were not an indication of an addiction, but a gift. I was surprised that he told the man that God Himself gave him this beautiful gift of sexuality. Unfortunately, James Tinney himself died at age 46 on June 12, 1988, from complications related to AIDS.[2],[3]

After Dr. Tinney died, Isaiah Poole and Michael Vanzant as well as Jackie Dennis became the overseeing Elders. They had an interim minister, David Morrow from 1990-1992. When he left, then from 1992 until 1994 Jackie Dennis and Michael Vanzant were the overseers of the church.

In July 1994, Doral Pulley became the next pastor, and he once preached for me at Community Gospel Church in Dayton. It was funny how, while staying in our home, Pulley was notably afraid (terrified) of our cat. But while together in our home, he told me that at Tinney's funeral all his relatives were Caucasian, as was Tinney himself. He explained that James was raised by a nanny who was an African American woman of color and who often took him with her to her Black Pentecostal church. He fell so in love with it and the people, from that point on insisted he, too, was a black Pentecostal man. No one challenged it when he said so, and only at his funeral did this get questioned. In other words, Tinney was black because he said he was black, even though none of his relatives appeared to be. But this was already news to his church at Faith Temple because he shared with his church that he was in fact Caucasian one year before he died. He said to his church that he was too white to be black but too black to be white. So, he self-identified as a black man in his heart.

Pastor Doral Pulley pastored until July of 1997 when he suddenly resigned by letter to the church and never returned to pastor Faith Temple. This was shocking and unexpected. But 7-8 years later Pastor Pulley returned to apologize for leaving so abruptly. Currently, Pastor Pulley pastors a church in Tampa, Florida. His departure deeply affected the church. They continued on, but not at the same level. As leaders in the church, and strong and honorable Christians, Michael Vanzant, Isaiah Poole, as well as faithful servant Jackie Dennis tried valiantly to keep the church together. Isaiah eventually moved away for college. Then it was

Dennis and Vanzant who kept things going. Beginning in 1997 they scheduled guest speakers to come in.

By 2000 the church felt they had been burned by having a singular Pastor and wanted a team approach. That was hard to find, but they finally settled in with Rev. Countess Clark, an ordained United Church of Christ minister, who also was an Airforce Chaplain. Another minister joined this team, Rev. Stephen Ford, and Michael Vanzant was part of the team. Ford did not work out for the church as they had hoped, and he resigned. The church moved forward with this team of Countess Clark and Michael Vanzant for quite a while.

From 1994 until COVID hit, they met at the New York Presbyterian church in Washington. But the second Sunday in March 2020, like so many churches, they had to stop physically meeting. In 2021, the Presbyterian church had new leadership, and like in the book of Exodus, where the new Pharaoh did not remember Joseph, this leadership did not remember Faith Temple and demanded that they come to get their belongings out of their building. Faith Temple has not returned to physical in-person services yet, but counselling and other ministry activities, weddings, funerals, etc. continue. As of June 30, 2022, they were deciding how to move forward, if at all.[4] This makes them the longest-lasting non-MCC, LGBT-affirming church.

[1] Picture from https://lgbtqreligiousarchives.org/profiles/ last accessed 1/1/2020

[2] http://lgbtran.org/Profile.aspx?ID=66 last accessed October 23, 2015

[3] http://www.faith-tele.com/2012_10_08_archive.html last accessed October 23, 2015

[4] June 30, 2022, Interview with Michael Vanzant.

Other Gays God Used

1st ' 5th Centuries A.D. unveiled by John Boswell

John Eastburn Boswell (March 20, 1947 – December 24, 1994) a Ph.D. from Harvard, was a historian and a full professor at Yale University and is perhaps best known for his 1980 book *Christianity, Social Tolerance, and Homosexuality: Gay People in Western Europe from the Beginning of the Christian era to the Fourteenth Century*,[1] which won the 1981 American Book Award for history. In this groundbreaking study of homosexuality in the Western world, Boswell argued against "the common idea that religious beliefs -- Christian or other -- have been the cause of intolerance in regard to gay people." He also claimed the existence of a highly developed "gay subculture" in Western Europe from the mid-eleventh to the mid-twelfth century.[2]

In 1994, Boswell published his second book, another exploration of homosexuality in history: *Same-Sex Unions in Premodern Europe*.[3] In this work, he argued that same-sex union ceremonies had become highly developed church rituals by the 12th century. Boswell likened these voluntary same-sex unions to heterosexual marriages and argued that they were entered into freely by male couples who desired to celebrate sacramentally their emotional bond with one another. While Boswell never claimed that all such ceremonies necessarily celebrated sexual relationships, he did not preclude the possibility that some of these relationships may, in fact, have had sexual components to them.[4] I mention him because his books changed the discussion around whether gays were actually heterosexuals making bad and sinful choices or whether they were born that way and that gay people have been known throughout the millennium. His books are scholarly and powerful. I recommend them to every LGBT Christian.

Prior to Rev. Troy Perry and the founding of the open and affirming MCC churches, God was still powerfully using gay people, though they remained deeply closeted; Lonnie Frisbee comes to mind. Much has already been written about Lonnie Frisbee and the documentary about him, *Frisbee: The Life and Death of a Hippie Preacher,* is worth owning[5] He was a young Hippie in the counterculture that God grabbed while he was high on LSD in the California mountains. He was also gay. But God used him to transform both the Calvary Chapel denomination with Chuck Smith and subsequently the Vineyard Churches with John Wimber Ministries. Both denominations later denounced him though they were transformed by his calling and anointing. Both denominations tried to write him out of their history (see the documentary: *the Life and Death of a Hippie Preacher*).[6] Nonetheless, God used him in dynamic ways as an evangelist, bringing thousands, yes, thousands of young people to Christ and baptizing crowds of young people in the Pacific Ocean. He operated in many of the gifts, including healing and prophecy, and functioned as an evangelist. His anointing was strong.

In the end, Lonnie was rejected by the churches he helped the most, because of his homosexuality. He died alone on March 12, 1993, from AIDS. He was 43.

Lonnie is buried on the grounds of the Chrystal Cathedral at Cathedral Memorial Gardens in Orange County California. Here we are praying for a release of his mantel to again be released in the LGBT community.

On one trip my husband and I made to California for the Glory Tabernacle-sponsored Charismatic Conference, we made a pilgrimage to Lonnie's grave. We felt that his anointing was cut short way too early, and just as Elisha asked for Elijah's anointing, so we too asked for his mantle to again be released within the LGBT community.

[1] Boswell, John E., *Christianity, Social Tolerance, and Homosexuality: Gay People in Western Europe from the Beginning of the Christian era to the Fourteenth Century*, University of Chicago Press, Jan 1981

[2] http://www.lgbtran.org/Profile.aspx?ID=138 last accessed October 17, 2015

[3] Boswell, John E., *Same Sex Unions in Premodern Europe, Vintage Publishing, NYC, NY, May 1995*

[4] http://www.amazon.com/Same-Sex-Unions-Premodern-Europe-Boswell/dp/0679751645, last accessed October 17, 2015

[5] http://www.lonniefrisbee.com/ last accessed 1/1/2020

[6] Ibid.

The Early Organizations and Conferences

TEN and Fred Pattison

PICTURE OF REV. FRED PATTISON FROM HIS FACEBOOK PAGE [1].

Fred Pattison was the pastor of one of the earliest MCC's. He pastored Casa de Cristo MCC in Phoenix, Arizona. He and his spouse, Joseph began attending the MCC in Phoenix in 1976, but beginning at Christmas of 1976, because the pastor was ill and home bound, Fred began preaching for them.

Preaching was not new for Fred. He was saved in November 1947 as a 15-year-old teenager while attending a Baptist church on Long Island, NY. Fred went to Bible college and then started his first church during his junior year. In 1957 while still pastoring, he worked with the New York Billy Graham Crusade. In 1958, he relocated to Tucson, Arizona, where he founded Faith Baptist Church. He pastored that Church until 1970. Fred was always faithful and a man of integrity; he showed long-term commitments to whatever he did for God. But in 1970 he realized he could no longer ignore that he was gay. His rigid and legalistic Baptist upbringing intensified an ongoing struggle with his sexuality. This struggle became so unbearable that he finally came to the belief that he had to leave pastoring. At that point in his life, Fred was unable to reconcile his Christian Faith with his sexual orientation.[2] He was not yet aware of God's new move to declare inclusively that God loves the world, including gay people. So, from 1970 until he and his spouse walked into Casa de Cristo MCC in Phoenix in 1976 Fred and Joseph Sombrio had no church home.

On the Easter of 1977 the home bound pastor of the Phoenix MCC returned to preach but then resigned, and on the first Sunday in October Fred Pattison was installed as their new pastor. The very next Sunday the old building that the congregation had purchased was firebombed. They rented a storefront until two years later when the church erected a new building at a different location; a building they now owned. Joseph headed up the building of the new structure. At that time, they were the very first gay-oriented outreach to build their own building.[3]

It was in this interim that I first met Fred. His congregation was meeting in the storefront when I first attended Casa de Cristo MCC. I first visited it when I moved to Phoenix in 1978. My spouse and I had recently moved to Phoenix from Pittsburgh PA after I had graduated from Nursing school. During the service Pastor, Fred announced that those who wished to help could come to the new site where they had purchased land and were about to lay the foundation for their own church building. Though they asked for help, in actuality, Joseph was overseeing and building this church facility pretty much by himself, without a contractor! He was remarkably talented. When the church was finished it was a breathtaking house of God. It had a Spanish motif and really resonated with the name Casa de Cristo. Other buildings were added to the campus, and they soon had their own printing press. This was important because Rev. Pattison was a prolific writer and defender of the faith. He was like a modern-day Martin Luther.

Because I had a new job as a nurse and had to work every other weekend, I was only able to attend a few times. Then in addition, especially because of the holidays, I began to miss my biological family and moved back to Detroit. Plus, the Lord spoke to me directly and told me He wanted me to move to Detroit to begin training for ministry. To do that, I knew I had to come out of the closet with my father, so I did. That didn't go so well, and he didn't want to speak to me or see me for over a year. But my mom and sisters were still my good friends, and since I had to obey God, I moved to Michigan from Arizona despite my father's objections. Subsequently, I never became a member of Casa de Cristo, and my infrequent visits seemed to keep Fred from actually getting to know my name or recognizing me when we met again several years later.

Fred was a solid Christian pastor, and very Biblically sound. He was dogmatic about his views of Christianity and did not tolerate variations of his views of theology. He was also clear that he did not like Pentecostalism, as he was trained and had previously been a Baptist minister. He carried the Baptist viewpoints with him. However, as the Holy Spirit kept moving within the LGBT community, raising up these churches, and filling them with His presence, Casa could not stay exclusively a Baptist-like church. The Holy Spirit brought in those whose Holy Spirit baptism was already evident, and they were enthusiastic in their worship and love of God. So, in a compromise, still not wanting to call himself or his church Pentecostal, Fred would print church literature stating that they were "Bapticostal".

Fred and his spouse, Joseph, were very engaged in ministry and the church was growing. As pastor of an MCC congregation Fred became involved in the denomination. Yet because of his rigid Baptist background, Fred often had theological differences with various points within MCC, and over time they became too large of a breach, and Casa de Cristo became an independent LGBT-affirming evangelical church.

"However, you must keep in mind that he was from a very rigid separatist fundamentalist background and being part of a denomination was new to him. He hates to admit it but Fred states he "became a thorn in the side of the leadership of MCC." He had carried over with him his fundamentalist mindset as well as his Baptist emphasis on autonomy and sovereignty of the local church. In retrospect, he says, "I created problems that I should not have." Fred is thankful to God for leading Brother Troy Perry to have the vision to launch out to the gay and lesbian community when he was a lone voice like the prophets of old. Fred said publically, "I am truly sorry for the discomfort and trouble that I caused my brother in Christ [4].""

In 1988 Fred began a new fellowship organization named TEN which stood for The Evangelical Network. In 2018 the network celebrated its 30th anniversary, and of those early organizations, is the only one still remaining [5]. "The original plan and purpose was to reach evangelicals within MCC. However, this never came to fruition. Plans changed because the church that Fred was pastoring, Casa de Cristo, called a special congregational meeting and the congregation voted to withdraw from the denomination. This decision affected the vision of TEN immediately because no longer was the original intent and purpose of the network the same. The networking now focused on reaching evangelicals that were not necessarily affiliated with the Universal Fellowship of Metropolitan Community Churches".[6]

So, in 1988, Casa de Cristo Church launched the first TEN Conferences. I had been pastoring Community Gospel Church in Dayton, Ohio since 1986, and in June 1989 we launched a new work, Community Gospel Church of Cincinnati. Fred heard of this work, and as the pastor of the church in Cincinnati, he invited me to come to Arizona, at their expense, to attend this early TEN conference. Casa de Cristo had also begun missionary outreach to a pastor/ overseer in Tanzania. They invited him as well. The conference was remarkable. By this time, our friend Dick Weaver, who had been instrumental in getting me to Houston in 1986 for the revival at Community Gospel Church of Houston, had now moved to Phoenix and was a part of this independent work at Casa. I stayed at Dick Weaver's home for the weekend. The pastor from Tanzania stayed with Joseph and Pastor Fred.

Fred took me out to lunch, to get to know me better, and it was here that I revealed that I had attended his church sporadically back in 1978. He really did not remember me. We hit it off and became friends at this point. During the conference, Fred asked me to say a few words. The Spirit really hit me, and I was led to declare that we needed to do a Jericho march around the building, and as we did, declare victory and breakthrough for our churches and communities. So, there we were marching and singing and shouting the victory as we went around Casa de Cristo seven times! You could feel a breakthrough was happening.

Then, I think as a courtesy, Fred had the pastor from Tanzania preach. Now even Fred did not know if this brother from Africa understood that almost everyone but himself was gay. We were apprehensive if he was going to start condemning gays or what! But we were polite and gave him full attention. It turns out he actually did understand that we were primarily LGBT folks, especially since he was being hosted in Pastor Fred and Joseph's home. But when he got up to preach, he did have an issue he felt compelled to rebuke us on: smoking cigarettes! Many of the leaders and conference attendees did smoke. And though no one smoked within the building, just outside the entrances were dozens of Christians creating a haze of tobacco smoke.

As the African minister got up to preach, he wore a sports coat. He kept opening it, as if to talk into the inside pocket, as though he was talking to Jesus in his heart. He would ask Jesus if He was still there. Jesus would answer: "Yes, I am still here". Then He would pretend to light up and smoke a cigarette. Then opening his coat jacket, He'd again ask Jesus if He was still there. Jesus would cough. Then a third time he asked Jesus if He was still there. No answer. He left. This was what impressed the minister from Tanzania about these American gay ministers. Several were smokers! His message made some of the smokers offended. But others realized that if that was what their witness was to outsiders, they needed to quit smoking, and did.

It was also at the TEN Conference in 1989 that I first met Rev. Lee Thompson and her spouse Rev. Yolande Yaeger. These two women have proved to be faithful movers and shakers in the Kingdom of God as well. Rev. Lee is an anointed prophet and apostle, while Rev. Yolande is a prophetic psalmist. When she leads in worship, you *are* going to have a Holy Spirit encounter. Period. They pastored a number of churches within the Grace Fellowship network and independent works.

"For many years thereafter the TEN Weekend was held the last weekend of February each year in the facilities of Casa de Cristo (the Phoenix church that Rev. Pattison pastored). The original Council consisted of a number of people (nearly all from non-MCC churches) such as the late Sylvia Pennington and the late Jerry Felix Russell. Cornerstone Fellowship, Casa's sister church in Tucson, with their pastor Rada Schaff, were all vital in TEN coming into existence. Soon an Annual Labor Day Weekend was held in Vancouver, British Columbia. Some of those ordained to the Gospel Ministry by TEN in its early years included: Rada Schaff of Tucson, Arizona; Jim Elsbury of Chicago, Illinois; and Rick Morcomb of Vancouver BC, Canada.

During those early years, TEN grew and thrived. Throughout the years, TEN has had a number of churches officially affiliated with it in the USA as well as in Canada. For a time, the Tanzania, East Africa group of churches were also affiliated.

As the founder of TEN Fred believed that there was a need for a school to equip and train others for public ministry. He founded Phoenix Evangelical Bible Institute (PHEBI) and headed it up until retiring and turning the school over to Dr. Joseph Pearson. The school is no longer located in Phoenix and has changed its name to Christ Evangelical Bible Institute and is a current affiliate of TEN.

In 1997, Fred Pattison retired as the pastor of Casa de Cristo Church and also resigned from the presidency of The Evangelical Network. Fred specifically requested that Todd Ferrell, an Elder from Freedom In Christ Church in San Francisco, consider taking over as President. Shortly after Fred's resignation, Todd was elected as President of TEN by the current affiliates."[7]

After his resignation and retirement from Casa, He and Joseph moved from Phoenix AZ to the little town of Strawberry, Arizona. Here he continued to write, and create pamphlets in defense of the affirming Gospel, had a newsletter, and as times changed, he had an electronic email newsletter. Fred was a prolific ambassador for God right up until the end.

As a result of a battle with bone cancer, he passed away to the sorrow of many on July 09, 2012. It was in December 1972 that he met Joseph Sombrio, who in May 1973 became his lover, companion, and spouse. Joseph remained at his side until the very end. Rev. Fred Pattison was a champion who left a large legacy in the LGBT community.

Under the leadership of Todd Ferrell, TEN began reaching out to Christian leaders within the larger Christian community for bridge-building within the Body of Christ. TEN began meeting with evangelical pastors from across the US, Canada, Africa, United Kingdom, and Australia initiating "safe, sane conversations" around the topic of homosexuality. As a result, many of these pastors have had to rethink their position on homosexuality and the Bible. Consequently, many of these pastors of megachurches have spoken at TEN conferences giving their dynamic testimonies of how they came to see God was indeed working within the LGBT community. TEN continues to be active in changing hearts and minds, one church, one pastor at a time.

Advance and Thomas Henry Hirsch

The first Advance: Ronnie Pigg "YOU have to get here!"

Rev. Thomas Hirsch, age 54, at our 20th anniversary at Community Gospel Church in Dayton, Ohio, July 2006

Rev. Thomas Henry Hirsch was the pastor of Circle of Glory, a Church in Ft. Worth, Texas. At 6 feet 1 inches, and a muscular 220 pounds, he was an imposing figure. He had a booming voice that commanded attention that sifted through his thick German

Rev. Thomas Hirsch

mustache. When Tom preached his blue eyes sparkled. Also, when he preached it was often for a few hours at a time as if he had to tell you everything he knew in one sitting. But he was so commanding and charismatic that no one wanted to miss a word. As Pastor Pam Ogilvie once said:

"You were fire and thunder and sugar and spice all at the same time...a life changer for so many!! We will never forget his prophetic cheesecake ministry!"

Cheesecake, yes, or pies of various sorts, for Thomas could cook with the best of them, and whenever he came to town to preach a revival, he took over the kitchen of his host and created meals that would be forever remembered. But in our case, I also remember all the flour all over the kitchen and the pots and pans I had to clean up. Nonetheless, it was worth it. Additionally, Tom's secular business, Phoenix Designs in Dallas, made draperies, pillows, and fabric creations of every kind, and thus he decorated Dallas homes and many hotel lobbies. He was very gifted. As a result, he also made banners and worship flags and gave them to churches when he came to minister. One church in Michigan had a storefront church and Thomas made magnificent floor-to-ceiling draperies for their windows. Additionally, at every Advance Conference that Thomas hosted all the attendees got a canvas, silk-screened bag with the conference logo on it. I have them all.

And so, it was when Thomas invited nearby churches for a gathering of like-minded saints to Circle of Glory in 1986, one of the pastors who attended was Rev. Ronnie Pigg of Community Gospel Church in Houston. After the revival ended,

Ronnie phoned me and said they are hosting another conference in six months and declared "You have to get here!"

Tom called his meetings "Advance" because, he said, we should never retreat, but only move forward!

The second Advance, six months later, at Circle of Glory Church in Ft. Worth, Texas, was again at the church Thomas pastored. Rev. Linda Harris, one of his staff clergies picked me up at the airport and led me to my host's home.

Some of the attendees included Linda Harris, also of Dallas; Rev. Ronnie Pigg of Houston and several other leaders. The Holy Spirit was particularly strong, and many prophecies came forth. I remember one woman bent over as if in the agony of labor, and the prophecy was that she was birthing a new ministry in the Spirit. Worship was intense, healings took place, and fellowship was established between Spirit-filled LGBT Christians. This was like a rocket taking off and there was no stopping it.

Community Gospel Fellowship had one more annual conference in 1987, which Thomas attended. At that time, he asked if we'd ordain him. Of course, we did, as well as the original founder of Community Gospel in Houston, Rev. Alvis Strickland and the other ministers who started new Community Gospel churches throughout the nation. But after going to Advance two to three times, we decided there was no reason to reinvent the wheel. As the clerk of the Community Gospel Fellowship, I wrote to all our churches that for 1988 we would all attend Advance and that would be our merged Annual conference. Thus, Advance, as an alliance of gay-affirming Spirit-Filled churches, was born.

Advance not only outgrew the facility of Circle of Glory, but Circle of Glory Church itself had several internal struggles and did not survive as a church. Many of the leaders of that group began other churches in the area, including Rev. Linda Harris, who joined Grace Fellowship of Dallas. The Advance conference, however, was off and running. It lasted twenty years.

Rev. Hirsch found a scenic campground in the Dallas area to host the conference. It began to reach 200 attendees. The problem with the campground was that it was really rustic. Really, really, rustic. The cabins were not heated or cooled, they were log cabins and held several bunkbeds in each sleeping area. All the bunk beds were twin beds, and they had partial saloon-type doors to bathrooms, and to the outside. Privacy didn't exist. That made it difficult for modest God-fearing Christians to work out routines of who could shower when — so we created a sign-up schedule. But also, for couples who were in a covenant relationship (remember there was no such thing as marriage for gay people then), there was no place to sleep together or have privacy. That wasn't happening.

It was the first year in this setting that Rev. Michael Cole of Long Beach, California, came. He was the overseer of several Christ Chapel churches in California and Colorado. He drove up in his big shiny Cadillac and wanted to know where his private room was located. Private room? There were no private rooms. We had six or more in a room. But Michael expected his own cabin with its own bathroom, nonetheless. I watched to see what Tom Hirsch was going to do about that. Michael drove his big white Cadillac up to the cabin meant for six people, where he was allowed to be the only resident. Well, imagine that. But, then again, he represented his own church denomination — Christ Chapel of Long Beach, California, Christ Chapel of North Hollywood, Christ Chapel of Laguna Hills, Christ Chapel of Palm Springs, California, and Christ Chapel Denver, Colorado. He oversaw them all with pastors ordained by him overseeing the various locations.

Michael Cole had been prophesied over that he would be a preacher at a young age. But after graduating from high school, he moved to San Francisco (ca. 1963) where he was able to live out his homosexual orientation that he had also realized at an early age. He moved to Los Angeles (ca. 1970) where he worked in the entertainment industry as well as studied at LIFE Bible College, in the Foursquare Gospel Church tradition. He moved to Long Beach (ca. 1974) and began a successful drag performance career as "Honey Carolina."

After hearing Troy Perry preach one Sunday, Cole decided to rededicate his life to God. Over the next few years, he played an active leadership role at the Metropolitan Community Churches in Long Beach and in Oceanside while continuing his drag performing. He later noted that he did not "feel worthy of being a pastor." After years of spiritual struggle, Cole retired Honey Carolina in 1981 and, that December, began a Bible study with seven people in his living room. This congregation steadily grew from his living room to his garage to a nearby storefront and finally, in 1984, to the current site of Christ Chapel in Long Beach. Cole noted that the hallmarks of Christ Chapel are that "we preach the Word" and "we're pretty much free-spirited in our music and worship [8]."

At this Advance conference, food was served in a common dining hall and a separate log cabin hall was set up as the sanctuary. No matter your mobility status, everyone had to go from cabin to dining hall, to sanctuary over dusty or muddy roads. That is everyone except Michael Cole. He drove his Cadillac from building to building. There were no walkways, just dirt paths. Yet worship was unforgettable, and God was very present as we entered into worship. Many gifts of the Spirit would manifest in those cabins among nature. The atmosphere was rustic, wooded, and highly charged with the Holy Spirit.

Because this was so powerful and life-changing, people asked Thomas Hirsch if they could have another conference in six months again, on the west coast. A site was selected for the outskirts of San Francisco. Tom had obtained a guest speaker, Rev. Sylvia Pennington. She was the author of two notable books: *But Lord They're Gay [9]* and *Good News for Modern Gays [10]*. She had been an Assemblies of God evangelist, who felt called to go to San Francisco to convert homosexuals into heterosexuals with the Gospel. Instead, she fell right into this affirming move of God and discovered God would not honor her agenda. Her two books were best-sellers.

But as I flew to California from Ohio, the Holy Spirit spoke to me and gave me a sermon. I wrote out my notes but thought this was strange since I wasn't a speaker and Sylvia was to be the main focus that weekend. But when we arrived at this campground in California, at the cliffs of the Pacific Ocean, Sylvia called that day to say she couldn't make it to the conference. There was a reason. Thomas Hirsch's philosophy was that the Body of Christ ought to *desire* fellowship. Thus, it was his practice not to pay anyone anything. You were invited, but you came on your own dime, and paid your own registration. In his mind, you were paid in fellowship and exposure to the Body. Not everyone agreed with this. Thus, the guest speaker wasn't coming. But this was also a way of testing who considered themselves a star, and who genuinely wanted to be with other believers.

Thomas announced to the group that Sylvia wasn't able to make it; and since he was cooking for the weekend, he did not intend to preach. He said: "Well, here you are a group of preachers, you figure it out". "You decide who will speak". It was decided that Michael Cole and I would each speak once. I was in awe of the Holy Spirit who prepared me ahead of time to preach that weekend. One of the honored guests was Rev. Elder Freda Smith. Unfortunately, she was not invited to speak, partly because she only came for one day from Sacramento to San Francisco, and additionally, since so many of these churches came out of MCC, I don't think they trusted what she might have to say. Among the conference attendees, there was a certain amount of animosity or mistrust towards MCC back then. However, Freda and I had a lovely time of fellowship together, and I was always thankful for how she so generously conducted my Holy Union with Robert when I pastored the MCC in Melbourne, Australia, and while Robert still lived in Ohio. It was a shame she did not get to minister because she would have bridged a gap between these churches and believers.

Since I tended to get up earlier than others, I took my Bible to read and pray outdoors, and while seated on a bench near a split rail fence, a brown fox jumped upon the fence and watched me for a while. Things like that always bless me. I always felt like it was a personal gift from God for Him to let me have a visit from one of His precious creatures.

That was the last time we had a meeting within the six-month time frame, and we went back to the rustic campground in Dallas on an annual basis. This next time, Michael Cole brought all his pastors along and many church members. His church numbered about 200 people, so he had many leaders who attended. Michael was very much a California guy. His clothes were impeccable, and his outfits were high-end and high style. It seemed silly to me to be walking on muddy roads in expensive matching shirts and trouser outfits. But that was Michael. I also found out why he insisted on having his own room. Part of his appearance, like his smile and hair, was not his own. He didn't want anyone to see him put in his dentures or hairpiece. It all came out in the end, so to speak. It seems Michael had many wigs because, as mentioned earlier, prior to pastoring, he was a successful drag queen named Honey Carolina

Michael was an important player in the building of Advance. After his first church was formed in Long Beach California in 1981, within the next ten years, other Christ Chapel congregations began: first in Denver, Laguna and North Hollywood ("the Valley"). Also, other Christ Chapel-related congregations were formed. When Michael Cole, the overseer of all these churches, gave his endorsement to Advance, all his other churches followed his lead. Michael was instrumental in the leading of those churches until his sudden death on March 25, 2005. Michael had heart trouble at the end of his life and needed a heart transplant. So, at the age of 61, Michael passed away, but his legacy and many of the Christ Chapel churches lived on.

Christ Chapel pastors; Left to right: Paul Doyle, Palm Springs; Judy Horn, Denver; Michael Cole, Long Beach; Jerrell Walls North Hollywood; Lilian Lobb, Laguna Beach CA.

The TEN and Advance Breach

To reach out to other groups within this LGBT affirming move of the Holy Spirit, Thomas invited Fred Pattison of TEN to come to Advance and be a guest speaker. Fred drove to Dallas from Phoenix and brought some of his TEN affiliates, including Rev. Rada Schaff of Tucson, AZ. Just prior to the worship service where Fred Pattison would preach, Fred became offended at the exuberant display of worship. Remember he had Baptist moorings and was not yet ready to enter into the full gospel charismatic worship of Advance. The worship service in which Fred was to preach was the afternoon service after lunch. But instead of going to lunch, he and his team packed their belongings and drove home. This was disconcerting since with no warning, the guest speaker was gone. This made a breach between the leadership of TEN and Advance for several years. Nonetheless, with the guest minister missing, the service turned into a powerful testimony time, in which almost everyone got up to declare the mighty things God was doing in their lives and home churches. Awesome, just awesome! The Holy Spirit wasn't slowed down one bit but took the opportunity to declare the mighty works of God around the nation.

And, in his defense, just as Fred apologized to MCC for causing them so much grief, because of his dogmatic stance; at the 10th anniversary of Advance, in 1998, Fred Pattison came to the Advance conference and publicly apologized to Tom Hirsch and to the Advance conference. It showed how much he and Thomas had grown. The breach had really only been between the two leaders. Yet as the Holy Spirit kept moving among His people, many of us cross-pollinated the TEN, Advance, and Spirit Fest Conferences. We were hungry for the presence of God, no matter whose banner was over the door.

After a few years, the Advance conference moved from the Dallas Campground to one outside of the Houston metro area, beyond the Houston International airport. This was another rustic campground but with nicer facilities. Still, we had bunkbeds, but since the showers had doors, people could take showers privately. Even so, we maintained the practice of setting up a schedule for shower use. The new cabins had a common room and two rooms for sleeping quarters off each end of the common room. Typically, men had one cabin building with both rooms and the living room, and women had another building. The food was provided by the camp owners in a spacious and sparkling clean dining hall. All the counters and kitchen area were stainless steel. Think concrete, stainless steel, and linoleum, rather than log cabins. The sanctuary was in a large, separate building. It easily accommodated the approximately two hundred people who worshiped there. One difference about this location was that the owners had a home onsite, at the entrance to the campground, and they did the cooking. Thus, when it was time to eat, we had to stop what we were doing and go to the dining hall. We had a schedule to keep for meals. On their property, the owners also owned a few 500-pound hogs; huge beasts, really. But we didn't see them while we were renting the campground. Not at first.

Because homosexuals were not welcome in so many places or facilities when negotiating contracts most of the time, our conferences were not identified as a gathering of gay folks and supporters, but merely as Christian gatherings. We were generally outed anyway, and in the case of this campground, once the owners knew we were gay, it was too late. They already knew we were Christians whom they loved.

The Mildred Wicks Fiasco

Pastors Sandy Schuster and Maddy Isaacson had an affirming church in Texas and became nearby neighbors to Mildred Wicks. Rev. Wicks was a famous healing evangelist in the 1950s and 60s. Born May 3, 1913, Mildred would make her way working as a field editor among many jobs within the ministry of Rev. Jack Coe Sr. From this ministry, it would be the launching board that would thrust her into a worldwide ministry that would take her to large auditoriums, and tent revivals, and she would become an author of many books during her 60+ years of ministry. Her name was mentioned among the other powerful healing evangelists of her time, such as Jack Coe, A.A. Allen, William Branham, and many others. She saw many miracles and saw many people get saved and filled with the Holy Spirit. When Sandy and Maddy met her, she was already an elderly lady and long since retired from the ministry. Sandy was an RN, and the two of them visited her often and helped her with various tasks. One day when Sandy outed Maddy and herself as a lesbian couple, Mildred already knew they were clearly Christian women. So over time, they invited Mildred to come to see what God was doing within the gay community.

Sandy brought her to the Advance conference in New Caney, Texas. When Thomas Hirsch knew she was coming he gave her a platform to preach. She asked for everyone with AIDS to come forward, and then she prayed for them. This would have been common in her heyday as a healing evangelist. Healing lines in the big tent revivals saw many documented miracles take place. But nothing happened either at that moment or subsequently. This caused a few of the gay men to conclude that God did not really love them; if this big-name healing evangelist who saw cancers and tumors and various illnesses all healed, but not their illnesses, it left their faith devastated.

During that conference in New Caney, Mildred met with all the pastors and leaders present. She suddenly turned to Dennis Schave and said, "You're a General!" She declared this also over Thomas Hirsch, Ronnie Pigg, and one or two others. That surprised me, not because the others were identified as the leaders that they clearly were, but because she completely ignored me, though I was sitting right there among these colleagues. It was, however, only one of the few times God actually let me know that I was not a leader at their level. I would hear this again, but this first time was surprising to me. This would be the one and only time we'd hear from Mildred Wicks. When the handful of gay guys expressed to Thomas their anguish over not being healed, Thomas's opinion turned sour towards Mildred as well as Sandy and Maddy. That caused a breach, thus Sandy and Maddy never again came to Advance. Mildred passed away July 13, 1998, at 85 years of age.

I remained good friends with Sandy and Maddy and since they pastored a church in Texas, occasionally they invited me to preach. They were both steeped deeply in the presence of the Holy Spirit. We always had a wonderful time in the Lord. I remember one such occasion after the sermon we had a healing line. A young woman asked for prayer for diabetes. Several years later she came up to me at another conference and asked if I remembered her. Actually, I didn't. But she went on to tell me that after I prayed for her diabetes, it was gone. And now several years later, her doctor still verifies that she is free from it. Thanks be to God!

The most memorable thing I recall about Pastor Schuster was a statement she gave me many years ago. Sandy is a registered nurse and worked in an office. A gay man got hired at her place of employment and was in an office near hers. It wasn't long before he transformed his office into a place of beauty with plants, paint, and lovely decorations. She noticed how so often gay guys just seemed to have a certain flair for making things beautiful, and she asked God about that. Why was that she asked? She said God answered her and said, "it was because He put Heaven in their heart." That made sense to me!

Sandy Schuster passed away way too early, in 2013, and Maddy kept on going. She made it to the Covenant Network conference in 2019 and was a blessing to so many. Maddy continues to minister in prisons. She mentioned that at one time, through her college, she administered GED exams to inmates. But now she gets to just love on them.

The Great Flood of 1994

ADVANCE CONFERENCE IN HOUSTON TEXAS, USA SHOWERS OF BLESSINGS!

63 CHRISTIAN LEADERS WERE AFFECTED BY OCTOBER HOUSTON FLOODS.

The annual national conference of Advance Christian Ministries was scheduled for October 17-23, 1994, and at least 180 confirmed registrations were received. Some people arrived early and began helping prepare for all those arrivals to Houston airports. The conference was scheduled to take place on the usually rented campground, in New Caney, Texas. Sleeping arrangements were dormitory style in bunk beds; each cabin initially was designated as a cabin for women or one for men. They all had two dormitory rooms, each with its own restroom and showers, and a common living room area with a snack bar and kitchenette.

The rain began Friday, October 14, before most of us arrived. It was a heavy torrential downpour that let up for only moments at a time, and then started up again. It was still raining on Sunday when most of the early arrivals were picking out the cabins they wanted to stay in.

Monday was an exciting day of anticipation; that evening was the kickoff service for the conference. Rented vans were busy making Houston airport runs and with each new arrival there were old and new Christian friends to greet and help get settled onto the campground. It was a time of great excitement at seeing so many dear friends, and also meeting new ones; of being affirmed as Christians and rejoicing with each other as we caught up on each other's news.

It was still raining.

While we were eating lunch in the cafeteria on Monday, the lazy little creek on either side of the only access road in or out of the campground swelled over its banks and over the deep dip in the road. The bridge over the creek was flooded. Within a very short time, those on the one side of the creek near the entrance to the campground had one building to themselves; on the same side as the owners' home was located. The water separated us from them and them from the rest of us on the campground. Thus, we had the entire acreage of the campground, its woods, trails, cabins, and cafeteria, but no access off-site. For a time, we still had phone communication, but that was soon to end.

People in the rustic wooden cabins nearest to the creek were instructed to join everyone else in one of the designated cabins on slightly higher ground and away from the creek. There were 40 people on the campground with no access out. The water flowing over the only access road was soon too deep to drive through for those who had cars. The dip in the road was too steep, and any car attempting to drive through it would have been up to its windows. Some of the group thought it was fun to frolic in the creek on the road, and even took advantage of the ability to wade through it to help carry supplies from the administration building over to the rest of the camp. There were 23 of our group stranded on the campground entrance side of the overflowing creek, where the administration building was located. Once it was obvious that the administration building was getting stranded by itself, with access roads out of the campground getting more and more encroached upon by the rising overflowing creek, those on the entrance side to the camp quickly gathered what they could into six cars and started out of the area to the Red Cross shelter, an elementary school building in New Caney,

Texas. Since the founder of Advance Christian Ministries, Rev. Thomas Hirsch was in the administration building and unable to reach those of us on the campground side, he appointed his board members to be the leaders and to give us instructions. That included Rev. Naomi Harvey, Pastor Michael Cole, and Pastor Ronnie Pigg.

The forty of us still within the campground had a worship service in the building that was designated as the sanctuary. It was a large, open, rustic, rectangular building with peaked wooden beams. In it, we set up all the sound system, the keyboards, the tape decks, and cameras to videotape the services, as well as all the metal folding chairs in tidy rows with a center aisle.

As soon as the worship service ended, the rain was still pouring down as it had been for days. It was obvious the creek was rapidly rising yet more and was quickly approaching the entrance to the sanctuary. The leaders instructed us to take one change of clothes, our toiletries, and our bedding and head to the one cabin furthest from the creek, and on the highest ground. The rest of our belongings, we were instructed, were to be placed on the top bunks of our current cabins. I obeyed the instructions, leaving a suitcase full of clothes on that upper bunk bed. Many others did not obey. Some left their dress suits and neckties hanging in the closets; Pastor Timothy Price of Agape Church in Columbia, Missouri left his laptop on top of a table in our original dorm's living room.

Those in our midst who had cars rode us and our backpacks, pillows, blankets, suitcases, briefcases, hairdryers, and mousse to our next refuge station.

Rain, rain, rain.

This was getting serious. One building was already flooded. It was dark outside. We were damp. Now, in one cabin, with the women in one room, and the men in the other, as soon as everyone got settled into our new cabin; we worshiped again. Then many went to sleep for the night. We had bunk beds. I took a lower bunk, and because the October Texas nights were cool, I had annually brought an electric blanket with me. I was about to plug it into the electric socket when I heard the Holy Spirit tell me not to. I argued momentarily, because I always used this blanket. But I soon realized God knew what He was talking about, and I obeyed.

Then I drifted off to sleep after a brief prayer. A handful of night owl preachers stayed up all night watching the rain, smoking cigarettes, and talking on the covered front porch. At 4 a.m. they came running into each side of the sleeping quarters, turned on the lights, and told all of us to get up because the river had now reached our cabin. No sooner did they say this than the water started rushing in under the exit doors from outside of the cabin. My flannel top sheet was partly dragging on the floor, and by the time I jumped out of bed, it was already soaking upriver water from the flood. I was grateful that I hadn't plugged in that electric blanket.

Meanwhile, out on the road back to New Caney, of the six cars that drove out of the campground toward the Red Cross shelter, only three had made it. The other three got to a point where the water had risen over the road in front of them, and they could go no further. As they tried to head the other way, another river swallowed up the road behind them. They spent the night as a caravan, driving forward from the river behind them and then backing up from the river in front of them, as the amount of available roadway they had kept shrinking. It took the occupants of this nomadic caravan until Tuesday to reach the shelter.

Tom Hirsch was among this group. When he finally reached the Red Cross shelter, he was told there were no survivors at our campground. You can't always trust the news, especially in a disaster. Another person trapped in one of the cars on the flooded road whose road surface kept shrinking smaller and smaller was Rev. Lillian Lobb, the pastor of Christ Chapel of Laguna Beach, California. Lillian was the proud mother of an adorable baby boy she had just adopted, and her new darling son was with her. When she arrived at the campground entrance, she assumed that for safety's sake Rev. Thomas Hirsch would tell everyone to go home, and be safe, because flooding was forecast along with even more rain. But Tom told everyone to stay put, and we would continue the conference as planned. But when Lillian and her son were trapped on a road, she lost all respect for Tom Hirsch and his leadership. When she was finally free, she got on a plane, headed home with her son, and terminated any further fellowship with Advance Christian Ministries. No one could blame her, putting her infant son at risk was just unthinkable to many.

In fact, because the flood kept getting worse, there were many other people scheduled to attend who never could get to the campground conference at all. Evangelists Dennis and Evelyn Schave were scheduled to arrive, but their Houston hosts, Rev. Chris and John Wellington were never able to get anywhere near the campground: roads were already closing off. Evelyn and Dennis had been staying in the Wellington's Houston home and preached a revival, the weekend before, at their church, Community Gospel of Houston. As they watched the news and the weather, they told Evelyn and Dennis, that if they could even get them to the campground, with all the flooding, they doubted if they could return to retrieve them. Rev. Chris called Thomas Hirsch, and since he had a large enough church building, offered Thomas to move the Advance conference to his church and his church members would host the conference attendees. Thomas refused the offer.

At 4 a.m. all the residents of the single cabin had jumped out of bed; we ran to the living room to be together and get further instructions. We thought boats were coming. We thought the National Guard was coming. We thought helicopters would soon hover overhead. We did what we knew to do. We began to worship. It must have sounded to any night creatures outside the way it did to the Philippian prisoners in Acts 16 as Paul and Silas worshiped in prison at midnight. The water rose within the cabin, inch by swirling inch. It lapped at the seat cushions of the couch in the living room. It got up to the level of the metal seats of our folding chairs, without covering the seats. Thus, you could sit on the back of the couch, with your feet resting on soggy cushions, or sit on top of the back of a metal chair with your feet on the seat. They would only get wet when someone walked by, creating waves.

The automobiles which had shuttled us to this higher ground were getting submerged little by little; they seemed like dying animals. When the water reached their electrical systems, some cars blinked their headlights on and off, and on and off, as if to cry for help. Then they shorted out and went dark altogether. River water swirled around their grills, then halfway up their doors. As one car after another died, there was no longer any escape. We were on the highest ground available. We could see that the previous cabins which we abandoned had water pouring into their windows.

We also had a few unexpected visitors. One was a snake spotted swimming in the knee-deep water of our living room. Those who first spotted it slithering in the water screamed! Some jumped onto the back of the waterlogged couch. But then there was Rev. Lois O'Neal from Houston. She said "Oh, for Heaven's sake, I'm an ol' cowgirl from way back", and with her white boots on, she stomped on the snake until he was no more.

Then came the pig; no, not Rev. Ronnie Pigg, who was also there, but a five hundred pound black and white hog. The owners of the campground, a husband and wife, whose house was submerged to the roof line, also had a few swine as livestock. I was told that one was named Big Pig, and the other was named Little Pig[11]. As the river rose, the husband went to the pens and released his animals, so they could escape and swim away if possible. This particular pig, Big Pig, took a trail through the woods and ended up in the water just outside our door. Each half of the cabin had an emergency exit, and on the men's side, we kept the door open so guys could urinate outside, in privacy just past the door. The bathrooms were flooded to just about three inches under the rim of the toilet seats. This also was the same level as the edge of the lower bunk mattresses. The pig sauntered on into the men's side of the cabin, and no one was going to stop him. He wasn't the friendliest pig, however. As he walked between the rows of bunk beds, when he saw a pillow (still dry) on a lower bunk, he grabbed it in his mouth, shook it violently as if to break its neck, and threw it into the flood waters. That ended any opportunity for any naps.

Rev. Doral Pulley, the new pastor of the gay African American church, Faith Temple in Washington DC, was on an upper bunk when the pig entered the room. He pulled the cover over his head and began screaming. "Get that demon out of here! Get that demon out of here!" He was serious and completely terrified. No one else thought the pig was demon-possessed, even if he did have bad manners. We let Doral know the pig was staying. Doral spent the rest of his time under the covers, screaming.

The pig neither left nor paid attention to the blood pleading, Jesus' Name invoking pastor on the upper bunk, hiding under the covers. But then again, a few months later, we had Pastor Doral preach at our church. He was afraid of our cat, Mrs. Cass, and insisted she be kept away and not be allowed in the same room as him. Along with Pastor Doral Pulley was Michael Vanzant, another elder at Faith Temple in Washington D.C. Doral made it clear that Michael was not to mention a word of this back home in D.C. He didn't until I asked him about it in 2022.

Eventually, the pig walked into the living room to see what was going on out there. Though he didn't have a demon, he did have the spirit of re-decoration. Lamps, tables, and gray metal folding chairs all got rearranged.

Another attendee to the conference was a guest from Columbia, South America that Tom Hirsch had invited. He was very nervous and didn't speak much English. However, one pastor from the Christ Chapel churches, Rev. Jerrell Walls of North Hollywood, California, could communicate with him and kept him comforted, holding his back tight against Jerrell's chest as they sat together on an upper bunk. They spoke in soft tones in Spanish, so they seemed content in their own little world.

While it was still night, there were no overhead helicopters, only black rain clouds, dumping out more showers. After a few hours, the husband who owned both the campground and the pigs, showed up, soaking wet, at our cabin door. He came wading through the flood, carefully sloshing where he knew the highest spots would be. He came to see if we were all okay. He was happy to see that Big Pig had made it to safety. Little Pig had drowned in that flood.

The owner was chilled to the bone and completely dripping wet. We offered him some dryer clothes, including a sweatshirt. He declined my only clean tee shirt which I offered him. I guess, even though soaking wet, he opted not to declare his gay pride. Well, it was the only shirt I had left.

But there was something else. Angels. They were everywhere. We couldn't see them, but in little ways, it was obvious we were being cared for. No one panicked, we joked, fellowshipped, and enjoyed each other's company, even if we were all standing in knee-deep murky water. For those who smoked, there was no need for an ashtray.

During our early predawn worship, we had an exhortation from the word of God from Isaiah 43:1-2.

Is 43:1-2

But now thus saith the Lord that created thee, O Jacob, and He that formed thee, O Israel, fear not: for I have redeemed thee, I have called thee by thy name; thou art mine. When thou passest through the waters, I will be with thee; and through the rivers, they shall not overflow thee. (KJV)

The Lord said He would redeem us.

After dawn and sometime near mid-morning a helicopter flew overhead. We wondered how we were going to get up to it. As we pondered how to get up to the helicopter should it lower a rope ladder, one woman, Joan Glascock, said, "I can't climb up onto that roof!"

I asked her what other options did she have? She had to reconsider. It was a one-story cabin, and the porch had a decorative grillwork that would function as a ladder if we needed to climb up to the roof. The helicopter didn't stay, it couldn't land. There was too much water, too many trees, and too many electric lines.

By this time water in the cabin was mid-calf or knee-deep, depending on how tall you were, but it did not get any deeper. We were thankful it didn't reach the electric plugs on the walls. It was still raining, but finally letting up a little. I understand that twenty-six inches of rain fell on Monday alone.

Around noon, we heard the motorboat. Two Christians, Stan and Dan, members of Peach Creek Baptist Church in New Caney, Texas, arrived at the cabin in the motorboat that one of them owned. By this time the water in the cabin had receded, and we had about a six-foot perimeter of soggy, muddy grass around the boundary of the cabin. The Lord said He would redeem us. These guys were not with the government, but private citizens, serving God, using the talents God gave them as well as the boat at their disposal to serve the Lord.

Their small motorboat could only hold four of us at a time, plus the two of them. The round-trip boat ride, to come and get the next load of passengers, took over an hour. Dan and Stan, as Christians, labored for over 12 hours, well into the night on Tuesday to see that all of us were rescued. I was in the last boatload. It was dark, Dan and Stan told us to keep our heads down, as we ducked just under electric power lines still attached at the tops of telephone poles, and under branches from the tops of tall trees. At the water line level, they seemed to be small shrubs. The boat followed the course of the little creek that had once trickled over our campground entrance roadway. But now the water was up to the roof line of the lower cabins that we had abandoned at the first and was still a raging flood, swirling around the cabins on the lower-level ground.

We reached the end of our journey at higher ground, which was a partially submerged roadway. Several more vans were awaiting our arrival to get us up to Peach Creek Baptist Church at the top of the hill. Once inside the church, we were offered dry clothing, including various kinds of shirts, trousers, underclothes, socks, shoes, and jackets. I had to abandon my search for an outfit to coordinate, though I tried. Thus, I had to settle for brown, dressy wingtip shoes, red and gray striped socks, khaki slacks, a tee shirt that said Peach Creek Baptist Church, and a jacket with a sports team logo that I didn't recognize; not that I'd ever recognize any sports team anyway.

Once clothed in warm, dry clothing, we were ushered into the many classrooms of the megachurch and slept in the hallways and Sunday school rooms off their fellowship hall. The Baptists fed us, and gave us clothing, bedding, and lots of love. We said grace with them and joined all our voices together as spontaneous worship broke out in our midst. But the Advance attendees weren't the only guests to spend the night. People whose homes and all worldly belongings were underwater were also with us, including a widow who had lost everything. It wasn't long before the gay pastors and Christians in our midst were ministering to her and other hurting folks among us. What rich fellowship. What a flow of the Spirit of God.

Once morning broke, several members of the Peach Creek Baptist Church of New Caney were making breakfast: waffles, pancakes, eggs, sausage, toast, and orange juice. This was no time to count your carbs. It was good food for hungry people.

One man in the kitchen, flipping pancakes, made some kind of anti-gay remark. Realizing we were a Christian group, he assumed we'd all have the same theological stance about that horrible monster, the so-called "gay agenda". He wasn't trying to be argumentative, but actually thought he was being friendly. I had only heard part of what he said, but still was surprised, in a disastrous time of tragedy, he'd even have that on his mind. Though I had not yet published my first book, *Openly Gay, Openly Christian, How the Bible Really is Gay Friendly*, I had nonetheless taught its contents in several churches. Thus, many in our group thought "Oh no, Kader is going to really let him have it!" They waited for my response. In fact, in the retelling of the story, some seemed to think I did set the man straight (so to speak!). But that wasn't the case. The Baptists were doing their best to serve the Lord, and us, in the process. I was thankful for all they were doing. This was neither the time nor the place for a great, contentious, theological debate. It also wasn't only me who was rescued, but many local people whose homes were lost, and some even had family who did not survive.

There were more pressing needs that day than to debate whether gays are ruining the American family. I had never found debates and arguments the way to win over human hearts. Instead, the contentious often dig into their position all the more. It is love that never fails. God tells us to love our enemies and to pray for those who persecute us. That was exactly what I did. I prayed for the fellow. Heaven knows I didn't want him to contaminate the pancakes!

Since no one responded to his comment, he picked up the non-verbal cues and changed subjects. Later, once I was home, I did write a letter to the Peach Creek Baptist Church, thanking them for their hospitality, and letting them know who we were and whom they had in their midst. There was never a response. Nonetheless, I prefer to remember the tireless good deeds of Dan and Stan, the clothing they provided, the feeding of the hungry, the rescuing of the perishing, more than recall the one sidebar remark of a man flipping pancakes.

On February 4, 2022, the former pastor of the Christ Chapel Church in Denver passed away. In her memory, on his Facebook page, Pastor Chuck Breckenridge wrote about her:

"This morning Rev. Judy Horn stepped into heaven. Many years ago, a group of minister friends and I were at a conference near Houston, TX when the waters rose, and we were caught in a flood ... after losing most of our belongings we were rescued by boat about 6 or 8 of us at a time.

Our group that was rescued that night after the sun had gone down arrived at the shore and was taken by van to the Baptist church where they had set up a shelter. We had been in knee-deep water for almost 24 hours in the cabin and my feet were freezing...

When we arrived at the church gym we were taken to chairs where we could sit and given blankets to wrap around us and warm us up ...

To this day I will never forget as I sat there Judy came and knelt in front of me ... removed my wet shoes and socks and put socks on me that had just come out of the dryer ... I have never experienced anything like this ... she was calm and loving and set the example of servanthood that night.

This was years and years ago and still, today if I put on a fresh pair of socks from the dryer I think of that moment and I remember my friend Judy. Please keep her wife of 39 years in your prayers (Darletta) ... Enjoy heaven, my friend ... now you know the secrets."

Meanwhile, back at the Red Cross shelter, the part of our group that was there was doing the same thing. They were feeding the elderly. The shelter at the school had around 300 homeless flood victims. The Christians from Advance jumped in to help the Red Cross; so much so, that the head of the Red Cross at our shelter told headquarters to stop sending her volunteers; she had all the help she could use from the "victims". Our people were unloading the trucks as they came in, helping to serve the food, staffing the phones throughout the middle of the night so the Red Cross staff could get some rest, and ministering in countless other ways.

Around noon on Tuesday, the Red Cross sent a school bus to the Peach Creek Baptist church and reunited us with the rest of our conference folks at the elementary school. They gave us our own classroom in the school, so we could all be together. The Advance conference continued on right there in the school. Some of the people also staying at the Red Cross school shelter joined us for worship. Who said there is no prayer in school? We slept on the carpeted concrete floors, and we kept on serving the flood victims of that community. It was also the first time many of us could telephone home. When I got through to my spouse, Robert Shisler, back in Dayton Ohio, he cried. He said he'd gotten a call from the Advance secretary, telling him none of us survived the flood on the campground. I was happy to put that rumor to rest!

The theme for the 1994 Advance was *"Go Into All The World"*.

God used the flood to give us a practical application of the theme. We were not able to stay cloistered and hidden and just read about the great commission and discuss it. We were forced to *do it!*

The flood waters had not fully receded at the campground, but the road to Walmart was dry. The Red Cross brought a school bus so those who wanted to purchase clothes, toiletries, or other incidentals could make a run to the store. One of our ministers, Rev. Michael Cole, from Christ Chapel of Long Beach, California always wore high-end designer clothes. He had never been to the likes of a Walmart. But he needed clothes, too. Once he was in the store, we could all hear him gasping out loud, "Look at these prices! This is so cheap! Wow, I need a few of these!" Poor fellow! Walmart was a culture shock for him. I never saw anyone buy so many pairs of underwear, shorts, tee shirts, socks, and other clothes in one store, in one shopping spree. His shopping cart was piled high! I was certain he wouldn't be able to keep under the airline luggage weight limits. In fact, he rented a car to go home to Long Beach.

Finally, the flood waters receded, and we were able to go back to the campground to salvage our belongings. We all had some things left behind in the first cabin we transferred from, plus the things left in the original sanctuary, as well as things in the registration, or administration buildings.

Thursday the buses rolled onto the campgrounds. Many of us, the vast majority, in fact, stayed until the scheduled end of the conference. We had learned the lessons well. The campground owners were devastated by the flood. Their small staff could not do at the same time what an additional 53 of us could do when doing it as unto the Lord and with a heart to serve.

The next several days were spent cleaning the muddy waters from the campground buildings. This included bringing all the furniture out to air or be hosed down, cleaning cabins, cleaning the kitchen and dining hall to make them usable again, and even cleaning the home of the camp owner, while they were still away. Pretty much everything smelled like bleach.

There were losses. But there were also lessons.

Pastor Chuck Breckenridge had brought his church's sound equipment and keyboard from Tulsa, Oklahoma. It had all been submerged in flood waters. Advance Christian Ministries also had all its sound equipment, tape decks, keyboard, and other electronic equipment submerged in flood waters, including a laser printer. The people with cars who had shuttled us to the highest ground all had their cars submerged to the windshields. Most of them were totaled. All those ministers whose suits were still hanging in the closets of the original cabins had wet, muddy, soggy dress clothes. And Pastor Tim Price's laptop still sat on the table on which he left it: drenched in river water. But even many of these Christians kept saying, "These are only material things". When the group was separated, some of that separation took place in households, with one spouse on one side of the river and the other still on the campground. Losing luggage and suits and clothing and even a personal computer or two paled by comparison to having reassurance your loved one was alive. Life took on a new perspective, and I don't think any of us could ever be the same. It was a life-changing, as well as a ministry-changing conference. However, it was notable, that those who obeyed the instructions of our elders, and put all our belongings on the top bunks in the cabins, came back to find everything dry and intact. The muddy river water reached up to the lip of the upper bunk mattress but did not go over the top mattresses themselves. So, anything left on an upper bunk was dry and spared from the flood.

There were heroes and heroines in our midst, too many to mention. There was great humor and fellowship as well. As our sister, Jackie Mallory, said at the Red Cross shelter, "It's hard to cop an attitude when you're wearing someone else's underwear!"

The greatest thing I will remember was the ministry: the Baptists to us; we to others, our going into all the world. And then there was the incredible worship. Hearts that are just filled with gratitude for a new lease on life cannot take God for granted. I thank God for the attitude adjustments I received and the things I learned. Some people had heard Advance was canceled that year. Not so. It was probably the most profound one ever, fraught with danger and faith. Hopefully, the lessons that were taught, and lived out that week, remain in our hearts as we go into all the world, in Jesus' love. Amen.

After the great flood of 1994, people were squeamish about returning to that campground and back to Houston. We finally agreed to go back one more time to support the owners of the once flooded campground. They were delighted to have us back. We went back still again in 1996. But since the owners had been devastated by the flood, they never quite recovered, and they put the campground up for sale after we had returned for the last time.

In 1996, the Advance Conference transitioned into the Alliance of Christian Churches, with 22 churches in the association of a fellowship. So, subsequently, the way the conference occurred was that a local associated church would take on the responsibility of finding a host hotel or similar conference accommodation in their city. They would offer to host, and then the leadership of Advance would help coordinate the next year's conference in that city. But it would be up to the host church to find a suitable location in their locale. I was one of the people on the board of the Alliance and joined in the task of this conference planning.

Sometimes, though, we were at a lovely hotel, and sometimes not so lovely. In 1997, though, we were back at another campground. This one was in the breathtaking mountains of Estes Park, Colorado. The Christ Chapel of the Rockies in Denver hosted this. It was a campground, yes, but breathtakingly beautiful. This is where I met Gerald Wright, and we became instant friends. He lived in Florida, and I lived with Robert in Ohio. But we'd still see each other several times a year at these kinds of conferences. We hosted a regional conference in Ohio as well, and Jerry would attend. So, he knew Robert, as well as other people from our local church. After I became widowed in 2005, Jerry Wright became my new husband. Yes, I really did meet Mr. Wright; and since all his siblings were boys, he is one of the Wright brothers.

There in Colorado, a huge brown moose walked right through the campground, unfazed by our human activity. It was also rumored that a mountain lion was somewhere nearby, but we never saw it.

I remember during that conference that the Holy Spirit was particularly strong. He convicted a few people to go home and start a church in Louisville, Kentucky. Thus, Open Door Fellowship was birthed. As that church was birthed out of the presence and Heart of God during that conference; Michele Troutman kept crying and saying when she got home to Kentucky, they had to have a church. Pam Ogilvie became their pastor, and it was off and running! Currently Pastor Sherry Roby is now the pastor, and she was one of the original founders when it got started that year.

In 1998 the Advance conference was held in Dallas, at White Rock church. It was hosted at the church itself since the facility could easily hold 500 people; and for 1999 the host city was going to be Philadelphia. However, the pastor, Jim Hensley, died suddenly from a heart attack so the conference was moved to Panama City, Florida.

The Panama City Conference. Tom Hirsch vs. Tom Gashlin, president.

I was on the board of Advance for many years. Churches offered to host the conference in their cities. In 1999, the Fall Advance was alternately planned to be in Panama City, Florida. Rev. Tom Gashlin had a church in that city that would serve as the host church. In order to determine the suitability for the conference, the board met in Panama City to survey the potential site. This was a gorgeous Sheraton on the beach. You opened your door, and the beach was at your front door. It was a breathtaking, world-class accommodation. Tom Gashlin was the president of the board that year. You could stay on the board forever, as long as you got along with Tom Hirsch, but he only allowed someone to be president of the board for one year. Tom Hirsch was like the CEO overseer and still outranked the President of the Advance board. But we had an excellent president in Tom Gashlin. He had wisdom, insight, and great ideas, and with this new location, the Sheraton, he really was helping to bring this organization up to a new level. It seemed silly and fruitless to me to keep electing a new president every year. I felt that if we had a good one, let them stay on and serve as long as they were willing and productive.

The board was the conference committee, and we met midyear in order to make decisions about the conference, sign contracts, or do whatever needed to get done to get the annual conference up and running. For some unknown reason, the most bizarre thing happened. Thomas Hirsch did not come to this midyear meeting. That had never happened before. Thomas was too controlling to ever miss a meeting of this type. But even without him, we held the meeting anyway. We had all travelled to Panama City from our respective cities and were already assembled. The Advance conference had also morphed into the Alliance of Christian Churches, which became an official affiliation of churches that supported this Advance conference. As a result, the conference also had a business meeting at the gathering of affiliated churches. At the midyear board meeting, we would also discuss any business proposals we might need the delegate churches to vote on. So, I proposed a bylaw change that we would no longer be constrained to changing the president every single year. Since Thomas Hirsch was not there, it was Tom Gashlin's responsibility as president to report to Thomas Hirsch what transpired at the meeting. When he did, Tom Hirsch made the assumption that this bylaw change was really an underhanded ploy to a power grab by Tom Gashlin and undermine Tom Hirsch's authority within Advance. Nothing could be further from the truth.

But Tom Hirsch was not one to be reasoned with. His mind was made up, and he went about to destroy Rev. Gashlin's reputation within Advance. I tried to intervene and explain that the bylaw proposal was not Rev. Gashlin's but mine and explain what my rationale was. Thomas wouldn't hear a word I said and went about making everything as miserable as possible for Tom Gashlin. By the time the Advance conference happened, the setting was beautiful, but the atmosphere was toxic. Tom Gashlin resigned before the conference happened, he really had no choice. So, there we were, having a conference in Tom Gashlin's hometown, but he wasn't welcome there. He snuck in anyway just to say hello to a few of us without attending any events. This was an unnecessary tragedy. A few ministers, who also loved Tom Gashlin, got the idea that somehow, I was on Tom Hirsch's side in this argument. I was not. It broke my heart. Tom Hirsch made up his mind and that was that.

But many saw how Tom Hirsch tried to slander Tom Gashlin's character and knew that Gashlin was not the power-hungry undermining person Hirsch made him out to be. As a result, many ministers just dropped out. I would have, it was times like this that I was so angry at Thomas Hirsch that I really wanted nothing more to do with him. But when I would decide I was never going back, the Holy Spirit would keep insisting that I stick it out. I did but wasn't happy about it. I would see, though, that if you looked beyond Tom Hirsch, you'd still see churches and brand-new ministers all looking for guidance and leadership. So, to obey the Holy Spirit and for the sake of these younger ministries, I stayed on. Despite such conflict, the Holy Spirit would still move on hungry hearts. A former Methodist pastor, Kathy Bauerle-Berg from Germantown, Maryland was present at the conference in Panama City. She came under conviction to leave her staff position with a church and begin an affirming church in her area. Thomas and his spouse Robin spent time with them in November 1999, praying, dreaming, and planning, and offered to help fund their startup costs.

October 10-14, 2001, the Advance conference was at a hotel in Wichita, Kansas.

This hotel was the most pathetic of any we had been to. The campgrounds were better. It was several hours drive from the airport; it was really dumpy as if it was about to be closed soon. There were not enough classrooms or rehearsal rooms for the scheduled programs. There was a restaurant on site, but the staff seemed clueless that there was a conference scheduled there, so there were not enough restaurant staff for the number of people at the conference. All in all, it was a disgrace as a location.

However, Open Door Fellowship became another one of the churches that joined the Alliance of Christian Churches, and Pastor Pam Ogilvie became instantly very engaged. She was a member of the Executive Committee (the Board). She was a powerful preacher with a strong, palpable anointing. At more than one conference, after an evening service was over, the anointing of the Holy Spirit was still present, and Pam would linger with those that were still hungry. At this time many would receive the baptism of the Holy Spirit or get a fresh touch from God.

In Wichita, people just followed Pam over to the hotel pool to get baptized. Although this was clearly God moving, Thomas Hirsch was not happy about these unauthorized extracurricular activities. He hadn't initiated them, and Thomas was big into control. So, this became an offense to him. Those who proposed these ideas would soon encounter his displeasure. He tried to curb or outright stop these kinds of things from happening. Once someone had offended Tom, he would never let it go. He couldn't stop people from going to the hotel pool in Wichita, after service, but he could undermine it in other ways. Pam had invited some friends who were under her mentorship. Tom had previously asked them to provide a children's ministry during a particular worship service that year. They were also recommended for Children's ministry by an appointed committee who also worked with them to make sure all arrangements were in order. But when it came time in the service for the children's ministry, Tom stepped forward and provided the children with a sermonette. The women he had invited previously brought all kinds of items to use in ministry to the children and this sudden undercutting of what they provided was highly insulting. I think it was intended to be. In a letter to the Executive committee (the Board) and to Thomas, Jill Andrews, the chair of the children's committee wrote of her deep disappointment in how this was handled. She wrote that the ladies, Monica Bly and Michelle Compton, "were most gracious in their disappointment and a great example of Jesus to me." (Submitted by Jill Andrews of Deerfield Beach, FL.)

The final blow for Advance — Tom Hirsch's arrest

Tom Hirsch was in a relationship with a man named Robin Gunter; all his previous lovers had died of complications from AIDS. In 2006 Advance was held in Seattle but Tom Hirsch did not attend. He sent greetings but said he had been in a car accident in which his car rolled over and subsequently he could not travel. Without Tom, the meeting fell into some chaos. There was no leadership with vision and direction. The next year, in 2007, Tom attended the meeting held in Dallas. But so did his lover, Robin, who asked to meet with the board privately. I was finally no longer on the board at this time. Robin showed them Tom's arrest record from both Dallas and Ft. Worth where he was arrested for soliciting sex with an undercover cop. He did not attend the conference in Seattle because he was under house arrest and not allowed to leave the area. Robin further showed where Tom was advertising on a gay sex site for bareback sex, even though he was HIV (+) and not indicating this on the website. They were able to log in and see some explicit pictures of Tom. They confronted Tom and asked him to step down.

He refused.

He tried to slander all the board, all of whom had integrity and credibility. Subsequently, and unanimously all the board resigned. More or less all of Advance exploded, and though Tom had some adherents who tried to conduct one more Advance conference, it flopped and another one was never held.

Because of this infidelity, Tom and Robin broke up. But for those who had not made it to the Advance conference when Tom was confronted, he made up stories. Tom told Rev. Adelle Barr that he broke up with Robin because Robin didn't accept his ministry, and that Robin gave him an ultimatum to choose either the ministry or him. He also told others many other stories that would not hold up to scrutiny.

I personally reviewed the arrest records, both from the Dallas TX Police Dept. and the Ft. Worth Police Dept.[12]

When Tom was arrested for indecent exposure and soliciting, if it had been in the 1970s, we probably would have picketed the police station, or the court, or marched in the streets. The early days were marked with overt gay activism as well as a general acceptance of this kind of promiscuity. But by the time this occurred, God had so moved in our midst, and we understood scriptures like James 3:1 where a leader is held to a higher standard, and the scriptures in Titus and Timothy such as "For a bishop must be blameless, as a steward of God, not self-willed, not quick-tempered, not given to wine, not violent, not greedy for money, but hospitable, a lover of what is good, sober-minded, just, holy, self-controlled, holding fast the faithful word as he has been taught, that he may be able, by sound doctrine, both to exhort and convict those who contradict." (Titus 1:7-9 NKJV)

A leader should be faithful to their spouse (Titus 1:6, 1 Timothy 3:2)

And 1 Timothy 3:7. "Moreover he must have a good testimony among those who are outside, lest he fall into reproach and the snare of the devil."

In the age of AIDS, we understood that promiscuous behavior was not God's standard for a Christian, much less a leader. And to make matters worse, Tom was openly soliciting unprotected sex, though he himself was HIV positive, and not disclosing this. It was his own spouse, Robin, who brought all this to the attention of the board and even showed them the website where Thomas was soliciting unprotected sex.

Tom died a few years later, on September 28, 2012, from a heart attack. His obituary read as follows:

Rev. Thomas Hirsch recently passed away from a heart attack. He was cremated in Dallas, and his family is coming Friday to take his ashes to their home state of North Dakota. Tom is remembered for pioneering one of the earliest Gay Affirming Christian gatherings in the United States. It started out in 1986 as Advance Christian Ministries and transformed into the Alliance of Christian Churches. The ministry reached people from as far away as Africa and South America, with support and labor for school mission work in the Dominican Republic. Tom had a successful business in Dallas called Phoenix Designs and with his staff and resources, he helped many new churches get off the ground and enhanced their appearance with beautiful banners, worship flags, altar ware, and even window draperies. Thomas led Advance and the Alliance for over 20 years. He always said we were to Advance and not retreat when we gathered as the Christian community. Thomas will long be remembered and his impact on goodwill certainly follows him. Rest in Peace to a true pioneer.

SpiritFest, Joshua Ministries, and Grace Fellowship in Christ Jesus

After receiving ministry in Atlanta from Rev. Tom Bigelow, Ken Coulter got a word from God to go start a Spirit-filled church in New Orleans. Ken Coulter moved to New Orleans and started Grace Fellowship of New Orleans. Here he met another early pioneer: Terry Enloe. Terry eventually became the pastor of Grace Fellowship in New Orleans after Ken moved to become the founding pastor of Grace Fellowship in Dallas, Texas. Initially, Terry moved with Ken to Dallas but returned to New Orleans to pastor Grace Fellowship there.

Rev. Ken Coulter started the church in Dallas and met in the home of two men, who were both named Bill. The couple had a large home in North Dallas, which provided an office for Grace Fellowship and a bedroom each for Rev. Ken and Terry Enloe. The large living room also had a church organ and several chairs and was spacious enough to conduct the worship service. Michael Bush was the treasurer.

But when one of the Bill's parents was coming to Dallas for a visit, and the couple was still very closeted; they gave the church a week to move out, before the parents arrived. That was the end of Grace Fellowship in that location. In the meantime, another member, Don Lewis was purchasing a four-bedroom home nearby in North Dallas, and as soon as he closed on the purchase, Grace Fellowship moved in.

Ken Coulter, Leon Linfoot, Don Lewis, Lee Thompson, and Yolande Yaeger, Linda Harris, Craig Franklin, and Tony Hoult were some of the earliest pioneers in those days.

Tony Hoult and Craig Franklin moved down with Rondah Kentch from Dallas to Austin in 1996 to start Kingdom Seekers, a part of the Grace Fellowship. Craig became the leader of Joshua Ministries in 1998 after Leon Linfoot in Dallas passed away, and later Tony Hoult became the president. Don Lewis took over Grace Fellowship in Dallas while Tony and Craig stayed in Austin until 2004 when they moved back to Dallas. At that point Lee and Yolande came to Austin. They reincorporated the church as Gathering Place Worship Center in 2005. They stayed in Austin until Feb 2008 when they moved to New Orleans, to pastor another Gathering Placed Worship Center church. Eric Hull was then installed as pastor as they were transitioning out.

When Community Gospel had its first General Conference in 1987, in Houston, Ken Coulter, and Terry Enloe attended. But there wasn't a "click" when we all considered merging. We respected each other and were all gay Pentecostal believers, yet it somehow seemed this was not a fit. Then, when Community Gospel chose to stop having its own general conferences but would all attend Advance instead, that was the end of any official fellowship. Grace Fellowship began their own conference called SpiritFest.

Ken Coulter died of AIDS. After Ken Coulter was no longer pastor of Grace Fellowship, next in line was Leon Linfoot. Pastor Leon was a man of integrity and highly respected. His spouse was Don Lewis. Once he became the pastor, part of Leon's vision was to see the Body of Christ, straight and gay, become joined together. This thinking was novel but certainly scriptural [13]. So, in the early days of the SpiritFest conference he invited many straight Christians to come and minister at the conference. This opened the door for many heterosexual Christians to see for themselves what God was doing with his LGBT children.

After Leon became the senior pastor, Linda Harris became a pastor on staff. One thing about Linda, she was known for her huge heart of mercy. She would be the first person at the bedside of someone dying of AIDS. This compassion of hers was widely known. She and Leon just did not see eye to eye on enough issues, so there was some contention between the two of them.

In 1985, Linda's mother died. As she left the hospital room after her mother's death, she encountered someone from the Dallas, Texas MCC (Agape MCC) in a room two doors down. She found this man in great distress because he thought God did not want him. His partner had called three churches in the Metroplex asking for clergy to come to the hospital and pray. No pastor came. Linda held him and told him of God's love for him. She asked him to share the love of Jesus by telling the next person that came into his room that "Jesus loves me, and Jesus loves them. Jesus died for me and for you." Soon a nurse came in. The young man cried as he told her that Jesus loves him, and Jesus loves her. Within the hour, the young man died in Linda's arms. Linda made a commitment right there and asked God to send her to those with AIDS that nobody else would go to.

For the next ten years, she worked through the ministries of Grace Fellowship In Christ Jesus in Dallas. She assisted the pastor there in doing many memorial services. She became an associate pastor with Leon Linfoot. But Leon did have AIDS. I remember him showing me lesions inside his mouth that were causing him great pain. Even though prayers, fasting, and intercession for him were fervent, nonetheless, Leon passed away.

After Leon Linfoot died, and as a result of the vacuum left by his leadership, it fell on his husband, Don Lewis, to become the next pastor, which was Pastor Linfoot's choice. But pastoring wasn't Don's calling. He really was a worshiper and musician and songwriter. He had a $25,000 Yamaha keyboard that he played as if an entire orchestra was present. He resounded trumpets and organs and strings and piano in a way that seriously carried you right into the heavenlies. There was no one like him.

Perhaps because of insecurities in being a senior pastor, Don Lewis asked Linda Harris to be his co-pastor. Linda Harris also engaged in ministries in other parts of the world--in 1995, she went to South Africa and ministered for six weeks as part of Joan Wakeford Ministries. She was a guest speaker at a women's conference in Vancouver, Canada.

Though feeling insecure as a pastor, Don carried on with his whole heart. God blessed him and he met the perfect help mate for him, Paul Revere. Don led worship and Paul is a remarkably gifted singer. Together they made a marvelous team. Plus, Paul also has a gift as a psalmist, so while Don would lead worship from that magnificent keyboard, Paul would prophesy and sing new songs of Heaven. It was truly amazing. Once they formed a union everyone could see how right this was. They were deeply in love.

There were times of contention between Don Lewis and Linda Harris. The contention eventually reached a crescendo, and Linda Harris left. Immediately thereafter, several friends asked Linda to be their pastor. They formed a new church called Sanctuary of Love. Harris was the long-time pastor for Sanctuary of Love Church where, church members said, she created "a ministry for outcasts, where love was unconditional. Because of that, people who wouldn't be accepted anywhere else would find love at Sanctuary of Love; and discover how to love others. Harris also played a role in founding or helping develop other LGBT-affirming congregations in the area. Her final ministry was with Rainbow Ministries International, which she founded after leaving Sanctuary of Love. Harris died on January 5, 2011, after a lengthy illness [14].

After Linda Harris's departure from Grace Fellowship in Dallas in 1999, Don Lewis was now the Senior pastor. Still, even with his musical gifts, pastoring was a burden. So, Don Lewis and Paul Revere resigned from the church, moved to California, and became musicians as part of Rev. Sandy Turnbull's team at Glory Tabernacle in Long Beach, California.

Grace Fellowship in Dallas then needed a pastor. Already pastoring in Austin, Rev. Tony Hoult took over the challenge of pastoring Grace Fellowship In Christ Jesus in Dallas, commuting weekly from Austin. Craig Franklin continued for a while as pastor in Austin. In the end Rev. Tony Hoult became the full-time pastor of Grace Fellowship in Dallas and eventually, once Lee and Yolande moved to New Orleans, a protégé, Eric Hull became the pastor of the Gathering Place in Austin.

1990s SpiritFest at Lake DeGray, AK

For many of the early years, SpiritFest was held at a beautiful retreat setting in Lake DeGray Arkansas, in the State Park in Bismark, AK. There the Holy Spirit did some unusual things. Since it was Rev. Leon Linfoot's vision to see the Body come together, he often invited heterosexual ministers to come and speak or sing. In addition to the Sunlights, he had Christian songwriter Karen Eagan minister as well.

One year, Leon Linfoot and Linda Harris invited Bob and Jan Bare, a heterosexual couple who had visited their church, to come to SpiritFest and check out what God was doing there. Bob got up to speak during one of the worship services, and as far as I know, he was the first heterosexual to ever ask the gay community to forgive him, (as a representative of the straight Christian community) for the harm they had done to us. This was a powerful testimony and a time of reconciliation.

Additionally, at that conference in 1997, there was a prophecy that came forth.

May 24, 1997, prophecy at SpiritFest (given through Rev. Samuel Kader)

You have thought that it was necessary to get my attention...to look your way, just to like you. You have no concept of what I am doing in your midst; what I am doing in your life; or what I am doing in your assembly. Grasp hold of My vision for you, My people. What I am doing is far greater than anything you can imagine. Have you not read that the last shall be first?

"I am pushing you to the forefront," saith the Lord.

While the church is running to and fro and while the church is trying to grasp a hold of Me: while the church is just waiting for Me to pass by and hoping that they can touch the hem of My garment. I am not with them, I am here!

I am busy pushing you to the forefront! And while they are saying "there is no place for you!" I am saying "I've made room for you!"

Have you not read in My Word where I said I would give you a name that was better than sons and daughters? Now, grant it, my sons and daughters have a wonderful name. Grasp that! I'm not giving you a measly, little piddly name in My Kingdom. I am giving you a name that is better than that of sons and daughters.

Who do you watch on television and appreciate their word? Who do you listen to their ministries, grasp hold of, and say "if only I had that kind of anointing?" How many times have you asked me for an anointing that was greater? Well, watch out! I am pushing you to the forefront. Now don't expect to stay in the closet! When I push you to the forefront the world will take notice! NBC, CBS, and Trinity Broadcasting will take notice! I said, "saith the Lord, that I am pushing you to the forefront!"

Have you not read in My Word where it says those who are least esteemed in the Body, to them He has given greater honor? So, I am giving you greater honor! Don't get smug with the rest of the Body and say "ha, ha, ha!" They're needed also. I've used them in your life. I've touched you with their ministries. Don't forget from whence you came. Don't forget how you got born again. Don't forget who first brought you the Gospel.

Take note! You are not second class. In fact, I am busy pushing you to the forefront. So, get ready! Because nothing you can do will stop Me! It has been My purpose from the foundation of the world. Now don't ask Me if I love you! Thank Me because of it.

This began to happen at Lake DeGray, the staff did not know, initially that the majority of SpiritFest attendees were gay Christians. In the early days, we knew people would not likely rent to gays, so we often just rented without telling; sort of a "don't ask, don't tell" scenario. So, because worship on site was so exuberant, often the staff would peek in to see what we were doing. It didn't take these savvy young folks long to figure out we were mostly gay. The next thing we knew a local Baptist pastor had been notified, and he too came to peek in to see what this was all about. After worship ended, this local minister in Arkansas asked if he could speak. He then gave a testimony of how he heard there were a bunch of homosexuals at the lake DeGray retreat location. He came to peek and scoff. But then, he testified the presence of God was so strong, he didn't know how, but God was here, with us! God had already said: "Now don't expect to stay in the closet!" Be prepared to be pushed forward!

At SpiritFest 2013; Rev. Evelyn Schave is preaching, while Pastor Tony Hoult of Grace Fellowship of Dallas is standing at the pulpit.

SpiritFest continued to be a dynamic flow of the Holy Spirit for many years. Worship was powerful and prophetic. In the latter years, it moved to the local church in Dallas: Grace Fellowship in Christ Jesus, whose facility was more than adequate to host this gathering. Pastor Tony Sirten of Nashville was generally on hand to cook, oversee the kitchen, and make sure all guests were well fed! He has an undisputed gift of hospitality. Jerry Wright, my spouse,[15] and I attended SpiritFest until 2013. We couldn't make it to the one in 2014 and after that the board of SpiritFest opted to stop having these conferences. Thus, an era ended of a particular flow of the Holy Spirit in the LGBT-affirming community. Though the SpiritFest conferences had ended, Grace Fellowship Church in Dallas continues under Rev. Hoult. Also, the Church in Austin maintained an annual Prayer conference. Rondah Kentch is famous in the community as an intercessor. Additionally, the church flows with her in that anointing.

Though SpiritFest had ended, yet more and more conferences kept springing up. At this particular SpiritFest in 2013 a guest speaker was Rev. Randy Morgan. He pastors a church of about 200 people called New Covenant Church of Atlanta. His church now hosts an annual conference called Immersed, typically held in July. About 500 people are found gathering together there to worship God in Spirit and in Truth. Though some earlier historical streams dried up, the Spirit of God is still flowing mightily in the LGBT community! Out of the Immersed conference was birthed the Covenant Network, a network of LGBT affirming full gospel churches [16]. Not only does the church host the annual conference in Atlanta, but they have a program seen on YouTube called The Covenant Network Broadcast. Many dynamic, Spirit-Filled speakers encourage the Body of Christ through this program.

RPI, Robert Morgan, Doug Clanton and Randy Duncan

SpiritFest really was primarily a Spirit-filled, Charismatic conference with people either already baptized in the Holy Spirit or soon receiving the baptism with the evidence of speaking in tongues, as well as other manifestations of the Holy Spirit. This became a powerful testimony to those who thought God hated gays. It was the same scriptural evidence as was revealed in Acts chapter ten when Peter discovered that God had moved out of His Jewish box and began filling Gentiles.

ACTS 10:44-48

> **44** While Peter was still speaking these words, the Holy Spirit fell upon all those who heard the word. **45** And those of the circumcision who believed were astonished, as many as came with Peter,

because the gift of the Holy Spirit had been poured out on the Gentiles also. **46** For they heard them speak with tongues and magnify God. Then Peter answered, **47** "Can anyone forbid water, that these should not be baptized who have received the Holy Spirit just as we have?" **48** And he commanded them to be baptized in the name of the Lord. (NKJV)

The prophecy was heavy, and the atmosphere of worship was intense. Yet, most of the believers were Trinitarian in the understanding of the Godhead, and for those who came out of Apostolic or Oneness backgrounds, this wasn't enough. So, in May of 1998 five Apostolic ministers, the reverends Douglas E. Clanton, William Randall Duncan, Daryl Goss, Michael Lawson and Robert L. Morgan met to form a new organization with a Oneness doctrinal stance, but with the desire "to create one affirming fellowship that would truly unite both Oneness and Trinitarian men and women who shared a passion for the Pentecostal message and worship"[17]. Thus, the organizing for Reconciling Pentecostals International began. In June 2000, two of these men, Douglas E. Clanton and Robert L. Morgan officially organized the Fellowship of Reconciling Pentecostals International.

The organization functioned for 2½ years under the auspices of Rev. Morgan's church, Potter's House Fellowship in Tampa, FL. In 2003, the RPI conference was held in Tampa and coincided with the fifth anniversary of Rev. Rob Morgan's Potter's House Fellowship church in Tampa, Florida.

I felt led to fly to Florida to attend this conference and was there at the time. This particular conference was highly covered by national and local media for a few reasons. Pastor Morgan had invited two controversial preachers of notoriety in the heterosexual Christian community to be guest speakers. How he ever got them to even come at all was remarkable. One was Tammy Faye (Bakker) Messner. She had a new book out [18]and after preaching she was there to sell and sign her books as well. Tammy Faye had long been a media personality, even if it was to make fun of her heavy make-up. In person it seemed she was wearing stage makeup. But as Tammy always said, (especially to Christians who would judge women for wearing make-up) "even an old barn needs a coat of paint once in a while". Her media attention, nonetheless, still brought attention to the Gospel of Jesus Christ, because that is what she preached. But the fact that she was at a predominately gay church made the national and local media show up with lights and cameras rolling. She had since divorced Jim Bakker, once he was incarcerated and was now married to Mr. Roe Messner. But her name was known around the world. It was THIS Tammy Faye.

Another speaker, also highly controversial, was Bishop Carlton Pearson from Tulsa, Oklahoma. He had pastored a mega-church with a regular television program broadcasting his services. The media was also there to see him, again, because what were these internationally famous ministers doing at a small, local, predominately homosexual church? This was news. November 14-16, 2003, was a historic event in Tampa, Florida.

Friday night at the opening service Bishop Carlton Pearson was the featured speaker. Pearson was presiding Bishop of over 500 churches and ministries through the AZUSA Interdenominational Fellowship of Christian Churches and Ministries, Inc., and has pastored Higher Dimensions Family Church in Tulsa, Oklahoma, for many years. He was well-known in Charismatic Christian circles.

But as of late, Carlton had been preaching a doctrine that was getting him in trouble with many evangelical Christians, and many people in his circle were distancing themselves from him. He was preaching from the many texts that say Jesus is the Savior of the world. But from those scriptures, he concluded that if Jesus saved the world, then everyone goes to Heaven in the end. This is the doctrine of Universalism (everyone is already saved whether they want Jesus or God or not). This is an incompatible doctrine with the Gospel of salvation through faith in the substitutionary cross of Christ at Calvary. He preached this again at Potter's House and there was an immediate negative reaction. However, the Christians there that night did not behave in any way other than being hospitable during the service or towards Rev. Pearson himself. But Pastor Robert Morgan who had brought him to Tampa had his phone ringing off the hook. He was the one left to defend the heresy he allowed to be preached in his pulpit.

The next morning there was already a planned roundtable breakfast discussion at the Wyndham hotel. By that time most people who had tossed and turned over this divergence from the basics of the gospel, realized they could love Carlton the person without embracing his theology or espousing it. This was something gay Christians had been expecting from heterosexual Christian leaders. We knew they may not agree with our particular take on the Bible but still had to acknowledge that LGBT believers are still a part of the Body of Christ. When he was not speaking on his controversial doctrine, Carlton Pearson actually was a very well-articulated friend to the gay Christian movement. He also had the long-standing friendship and the ear of major Christian leaders, such as Oral Roberts, in Tulsa. This access he had to other high-profile Christians in itself made us think we would probably be seeing him again. Even if his doctrine was not going to get a wide audience, his openness to gay Christians and indeed to gays, in general, was too compelling to ignore. People wanted to hear for themselves what he had to say.

However, Pearson's universalist doctrinal stance was already branding him a heretic. Then, added to this; he theologically embraced gay people, which made him completely rejected. The Christian News media made it plain he was not welcome in their camp:

One report went like this:

On March 7th of 2002, Charisma News Service announced that Carlton Pearson, a well-known Charismatic preacher in Tulsa, OK, and frequent minister on TBN, (Trinity Broadcasting Network) had a different gospel. Pearson said that he knew some of his views-- such as his belief that homosexuality should be "tolerated but not celebrated"--would raise some eyebrows, the newspaper said. "The religious folk wants these people to go to hell," he said. After that announcement Pearson's doctrine was denounced: Three well-known black Pentecostal preachers denounced Tulsa, Okla., pastor Carlton Pearson's "Gospel of Inclusion," which questions the existence of a literal hell and espouses that everyone is already saved. (CNS 3-27-02) The three were Bishop Charles Blake, pastor of West Angeles

(Calif.) Church of God in Christ (COGIC), and Bishop G.E. Patterson, head of COGIC, and T.D. Jakes. Blake and Patterson have dismissed "any knowledge or support of Pearson's doctrine." And Jakes said he *"emphatically and unequivocally" repudiated inclusionism -- also known as universalism -- as "heresy." (CNS 3-27-02)* Despite a mass exodus of his congregation and a large drop in numbers at his annual Azusa summer conference, Bishop Carlton Pearson of Tulsa, Okla., has said he will stand by his commitment to preach a "more appealing and attractive message of God's unconditional love for all." . . . Although he does not like the term "inclusion," Pearson said he does believe that Jesus' death and resurrection paid the price for all the world to spend eternal life in heaven, without the requirement that people repent, confess and receive their salvation. (CNS 9-6-02) Pearson is not the only one that preaches that message; it has been around a long time and is called, "Universal Reconciliationism" or just "Universalism." They believe that Muslims, Hindus, Buddhists, and Unitarians -- will go to heaven.

Even though Pearson is not a member of the World Bishops Council (WBC), he agreed to appear before them to have his doctrine examined. In November, they declared him to be a heretic. "We issued a correction of the teachings and have clearly stated that we cannot support the gospel of inclusion as it stands," WBC president Timothy Paul Baymon told Charisma News Service. Baymon noted that the decision was based on the Canons of the Altogether Apostles, which have been used for centuries. (CNS 11-18-02) [19]

Another notable figure at the roundtable was going to be that night's speaker, Rev. D.E. [Donnie Earl] Paulk of Atlanta. His father and uncle had pioneered the 15,000-member Cathedral at Chapel Hill Church in Decatur, Georgia (near Atlanta). Recently D.E. became the senior pastor of this church in the Atlanta area. At the time of this conference, he had started his own new gay-friendly church and it was only five weeks old. He reported then that it had doubled in size to 200 people. D.E. was very personable and comfortable among his gay brothers and sisters.

Unfortunately, when D.E. Paulk preached, he too brought forth his own version of universalism.

The other leaders of RPI would not tolerate this heresy in their midst and wanted Rev. Rob Morgan to explain himself. He said to me that he didn't know what they were actually going to preach and was as surprised as everyone else that they brought this up in their sermons. Nonetheless, this brought about a breach within RPI, and Rob Morgan was no longer a part of the fellowship.

Now, oddly enough, not just secular media was there, but so was Christian media.

In April 2004 Charisma Magazine reported that they had a "spy" at the Tampa meeting. From their website they reported:

First Word

Heretics Among Us

By J. Lee Grady

Last fall I was shocked to learn that a group of charismatic church leaders were convening in Tampa, Florida, to discuss ways they could promote a homosexual agenda. I thought only Episcopalians were sliding in this direction, so I sent an undercover reporter to the meeting. She sat in the back of the room and listened while these leaders suggested ways to spread their unorthodox message.

They met in a "gay-affirming" church led by a former Assembly of God minister. Attendees included Oklahoma-based pastor Carlton Pearson, who made headlines last year when he announced that he had adopted a more "inclusive" theology. Pearson already believes everyone is saved, yet now he has stepped into deeper doctrinal quicksand with the idea that unrepentant homosexuals will get a free ticket to heaven.

Pearson said he hoped gay leaders would "build silent bridges" by joining the staffs of "heterosexual churches" and gradually convincing them to accept the gay lifestyle. Another pastor told the group:

"We do not believe that loving someone of the same sex in a committed, monogamous relationship is a sin."

Did you ever imagine we would see a day when so-called Spirit-filled ministers would call for the open acceptance of sexual perversion? If you can't hear the alarm bell buzzing, please have your ears checked. We need to pull our heads out of the sand and recognize that the American church is racing toward the biggest culture clash of our time.[20]

I had a subscription to Charisma magazine at the time, and when this article came out, I was seriously disappointed. They had a spy in our midst? Why would they need one? We were not the enemy. And it was not only Carlton Pearson and D. E. Paulk who spoke. Yes, they brought their unorthodox but gay-friendly message, but that was merely a diversion from the main point. Many people shared actual truth and revelation from God at that meeting. One of those was Tammy Faye Bakker Messner. Her message was so powerful that even the secular media were weeping and drying their eyes.

Tammy Faye [Bakker] Messner

With the news media there in full force and cameras rolling, Tammy Faye [Bakker] Messner preached the Sunday morning service and brought a message of healing and forgiveness. She related the story of how she and her former husband Jim Bakker lost the entire PTL [Praise the Lord] TV empire. Richard Dortch [*How I Lost My Integrity and Got It Back*][21] reported how evangelical leader Jerry Falwell maneuvered that network station out of the Bakker's hands. Tammy Faye preached how it took her a long time to forgive Jerry Falwell for that event. But she gave a formula for forgiving anyone who hurts you deeply. She told a story about ancient times. Then, when a person had murdered someone, they were not just put to death. Instead, she said, they would strap the corpse of the person you murdered to your back. [Possible where we get the saying

"Get off my back!"] As the corpse was filling with maggots and decaying, no one would get near you for the stench. You would also find it hard to eat with the putrefaction going on.

Additionally, as the body bloated, it became heavier to carry. She realized that carrying a grudge was like carrying this corpse behind you. It doesn't affect the person who hurt you, but it does affect you. Unforgiveness, carrying this burden around all the time, could eventually kill you. She decided not to let someone have that much power over her life.

Tammy Faye said she made a decision to stand up and unbuckle the belt that kept Jerry Falwell strapped to her back and drop the corpse. Just let it go and move forward. She told people in the church who were hurting from past events to stand up and, at her direction; symbolically unbuckled the belt and let the issue fall to the ground: releasing them to freedom. So many corpses fell that day!

So many gay people had been hurt by the church world and were carrying around pain and bitterness. Charisma magazine wasn't helping. But at Tammy Faye's leadership, we let it go! We were free from what others had said or done. As I said, even the cameramen and reporters were in tears. The Holy Spirit was powerfully moving at that service.

Also, during that service, while Tammy was leading people in prayer for forgiveness, a man named Dave from Michigan got baptized in Holy Spirit and had a release of his prayer language. Tammy Faye did not know this. The next day several of us took him to Tampa's airport Wyndham hotel pool on the 9th floor and baptized him in water. Rev. C. J. Michaels took him in the water and Rev. Linda Harris of Dallas, Paul Parnell from Indianapolis, and I were all witnesses to the event.

When the Sunday morning service had ended, Tammy Faye and her husband; architect and builder, Ro Messner, were in the lobby of the church as she autographed copies of her new book: *I Will Survive... and You Can, Too!* [22]

After the conference ended, most people flew out on Monday. There in the Tampa airport, I met Ro Messner, Tammy Faye's husband, and later saw Tammy there as well.

I told her how Dave had been baptized in the Holy Spirit while she was preaching; exactly as it happened in the book of Acts, chapter 10; when Peter was preaching to "those people" the Roman occupational forces, Cornelius, and his household.

I saw Tammy Faye Bakker Messner one more time before she died of cancer. But that story comes later.

After the Charisma article appeared in 2004, Pastor Rob Morgan responded in the most loving way to their homophobia. And before he did, he wrote to other leaders in this affirming movement to see if his tone and statements were acceptable, willing to accept correction before he sent out his response. Rob Morgan wrote:

Dear Mr. Strang and Mr. Grady,

I greet you in the Name above all names to address your recent negative reference to me and the church family that God and I birthed almost six years ago. I would ask you in the future to please verify your information before publishing it as truth. Let me set the record straight on a few points you made. The purpose of our meeting was NOT to discuss ways to promote a homosexual agenda but rather how we could build bridges of fellowship with other affirming ministries like ours, as well as non-affirming ministries. You didn't send an undercover reporter. I called Charisma twice and informed you about our gathering so that you could come by invitation. We had a very diverse group at the roundtable discussion and a number of things were voiced that not everyone agreed with, such as Bishop Pearson's views on inclusive theology. Although I was raised in the Assemblies of God, I was never licensed with the A/G, but rather the United Pentecostal Church International. Your attempt to vilify us appears to be purely negative propaganda.

The Scriptures say to speak the truth in love. Your article, "Heretics Among Us" contained neither truth nor love. I want my letter to be full of both. Truth illuminates and sets people free, which is what happens in our church when God is allowed to open a mind that has been filled with the darkness of misinterpreted, misapplied passages of Scripture and fear, an ignorance-based myth. Truth sets people free when their God-created sexual orientation is reconciled with the pure Word of God and an ever-increasing social and scientific understanding regarding the subject of sexual orientation. It is the tradition-bound church that presently puts trusting, gay Christians in bondage and torment. As in the past, the church eventually, clumsily and reluctantly accepts the light of liberating truth (Biblical and scientific) but sadly, not until the spiritual carnage has reached enormous proportions. That's why, to the church's embarrassment, most modern believers now admit that we were wrong in previous stands we took and accept as fact that the world is round, women are equal, and slavery is wrong. Can we not look at history and see a pattern here? I fear our reputation in the world is terribly well deserved. Rather than lovingly lead this world to complete truth and enlightenment on this subject, once again Christians appear silly as they run around screaming that the sky is falling.

It is straight, evangelical parents and churches who put their children in my church pews every Sunday because they are viewed by their gay offspring, as well as our world, to be the Pharisees of our day toward the very people Jesus came to touch and save. The church's party line on this issue has been horribly destructive, spiritually and psychologically. No doubt Jesus would have a lot to say to the white-washed sepulchers of our day. The hypocrisy and double standards seen in the church, by the world on this and other issues, are appalling. Many of your own pastors and right-wing politicians are in their second and third marriages. It appears that you could use our help to preserve the institution of marriage. This sad situation is compounded by constant hateful and angry rhetoric spewed out by pastors, such as the one on your April cover. Why does the evangelical church always need an enemy they can beat up on? This, in the light of the church's preoccupation with glitz rather than glory, turns already wounded hearts away from your ranks and into the world. We are able to salvage a few who come in longing for the Presence of God. They just can't bear more of your failed, hocus-pocus, trying to fix a sexual orientation that doesn't need fixing. Articles like yours force hurting, struggling souls deeper into despair and condemnation, into the world, away from God's Presence, and eventually, into eternity without hope.

The love we preach is not mushy, as you put it. It's tangible! It's the only thing that can heal the wounds the Body of Christ as inflicted on its own children. My church's love for these searching hearts has to be strong to continue loving, reaching, and praying while you and others continue your barrage of negative propaganda. There are millions of gay men and women in this world, many of whom you rub elbows within the church every day and you don't even realize it. The church has obviously not found an effective means of reaching them so until you do, please be slow to judge those of us who are reaching them and seeing their wounds healed.

We are committed to loving you, praying for you, and serving you as we find opportunity, simply because the love of God constrains us to do so. It is no one's place to determine who is a tare and should thus be separated from those deemed to be wheat. The Lord knows them that are His and it is our place to love unconditionally and leave judgment to Him.

We have no agenda but evangelism, no goal but the glory of God, and apparently (among our Spirit-filled brothers and sisters), no support but the grace-filled grip of nail-scarred hands. I highly recommend a less condescending approach to this subject, at least until you can legitimately claim to have all the scientific facts on the complicated subject of human sexuality. Your column is titled "First Word", but God will have the last word as to our salvation. Our trust is in Him alone and His finished work on Calvary. "After the way called heresy, so worship I the God of my fathers."

Pastor Robert L. Morgan

Potter's House Fellowship, Tampa, FL

Pastor Rob Morgan no longer pastors, but his church, Potter's House still lives on. It has changed its name to Connection Church Tampa Bay in Tampa, Florida,[23] and had been pastored by Rev. Steve Andrews for many years after that. It is currently pastored by Rev. Kelsey Swope. Also, RPI is alive and well and their annual dynamic conference is still going on. The leadership has some incredible, honorable, and anointed people of integrity. Pastor Randy Duncan who pastors New Life Connect Point in LaPorte, Indiana, and Rev. Doug Clanton who pastors Reconciling Pentecostal Assembly in Phoenix Arizona remain among the leadership of the original organization.

The Fellowship of Reconciling Pentecostals is presently headquartered in La Porte, Indiana.[24]

RPI General Conference in LaPorte Indiana. Of note are Bishop Randy Duncan (L) and his spouse Dan Wright (R) at the podium; Pastor Sandy Turnbull (R) pastor of Glory Tabernacle of Long Beach, CA; and her spouse, Janet Robertson (L) on the far-left front row. I am the rebel in the blue green sweatshirt, second row next to Rev. Sandy Turnbull.

[1] https://www.facebook.com/frederick.pattison last accessed December 25, 2019

[2] https://4a0916f5-d23e-4165-87a0-2db45f5cc637.filesusr.com/ugd/4b5da2_31186e373cb14e6eb431de12dad89092.pdf

Last accessed December 25, 2019

[3] ibid

[4] ibid

[5] https://www.ten.lgbt/ last accessed 12/30/2019

[6] ibid

[7] ibid

[8] http://lgbtran.org/Interview.aspx?ID=2 last accessed December 3, 2015

[9] Pennington, Sylvia, *But Lord They're Gay* Lambda Christian Fellowship, Hawthorne, CA, 1982

[10] Pennington, Sylvia, *Good News for Modern Gays* Lambda Christian Fellowship, Hawthorne, CA, 1985

[11] June 20, 2022, Interview with Michael Vanzant

[12] https://records.txdps.state.tx.us/DpsWebsite/CriminalHistory/Application/Search/Individual.aspx?BatchId=3177577&SearchId=13859666&IND_IDN=2774550&ShowPreview=False LAST ACCESSED December 2, 2015.

[13] John 17: 20-21; Ephesians 2: 14-22.

[17] http://lgbtran.org/Profile.aspx?ID=288 last accessed December 3, 2015

[15] (Robert Shisler, my previous spouse of twenty years died in 2005)

[16] www.thecovenantnetwork.com (last accessed 6/21/2022)

[17] http://www.rpifellowship.com/ last accessed 12/30/2019

[18] Messner, Tammy Faye, *I Will Survive and You Will Too!* Tarcher Perigee, Los Angeles CA, Sept. 2003

[19] http://www.firefromheaven.net/2003/apostasy-pearson.html

[20] http://www.charismamag.com/articledisplay.pl/?ArticleID=8673

[21] Dortch, Richard, *How I Lost My Integrity And Got It Back*, New Leaf Press, Green Forrest AK, 1993.

[22] Messner, Tammy Faye, *I Will Survive and You Will Too!* Tarcher Perigee, Los Angeles CA, Sept. 2003

[23] https://www.connectionchurchtb.com/about-us last accessed July 25, 2022

[24] https://rpifellowship.com/about-us last accessed July 25, 2022

Charismatic Conference — Harvest Glory — All Nations' Conference

Dusty Pruitt, then Sandra Turnbull

Rev. Dusty Pruitt was born on July 19, 1946, in Ballinger, Texas, the firstborn of three sisters, one 15 months younger and the other 12 years younger. Dusty grew up in Bronte, Texas, a town of just under 1,000 people in west-central Texas. Her father was a World War II bomber crewman, who completed 35 missions over Germany before coming home. The family moved to Fort Sam Houston, Texas, when her father's reserve unit was activated during the Korean War. Dusty's father became a Baptist minister for the Baptist Missionary Association when she was six. This began a moving saga in which she attended ten different schools before she graduated at age 17 from high school.

She earned an Associate of Arts degree from Jacksonville Baptist College in Jacksonville, Texas, in 1965. Then she attended the University of Texas at Arlington and graduated in 1970 from Stephen F. Austin State University in Nacogdoches, Texas, with a Bachelor of Arts degree in English and Spanish with a minor in Education.

Pruitt entered the Army as a second lieutenant in 1970. There she came to understand that she was gay. She met Sgt. Sandy McMillan in 1971, and thus was introduced to Metropolitan Community Church in Atlanta, Georgia. After being transferred to Army Recruiting in Dallas, Texas, Pruitt joined Agape MCC in Fort Worth, Texas, in 1972 as a charter member.

She was transferred from Army active duty to the Reserves in 1976 and began studying at the Iliff School of Theology in Denver, Colorado. In 1980, she became the first openly LGBT person to graduate with a Master of Divinity degree from that school. She began pastoring the Metropolitan Community Church in Long Beach, California, where she pastored for 15 years, until 1995.

In 1983, after pastoring MCC Long Beach for three years and continuing to drill with the Army Reserve two times a month and two weeks a year, she gave an interview to the *Los Angeles Times (August 1991)* [1] about her work with MCC as an example of how one person could reconcile the often-wrenching conflict, many gay men and lesbians feel between their being gay and loving God. This article was picked up by Pruitt's commander in the Individual Ready Reserve who initiated an investigation into Pruitt's moral character (for being gay). This investigation took away her promotion to Major and gave her an honorable discharge. Pruitt went to the American Civil Liberties Union, which took her case along with the Lambda Legal Defense and Education Fund. The ensuing 12-year legal battle was resolved in 1995 with Pruitt's being reinstated, accorded the promotion to Major, and then retired with the Army Reserves [2]. The case was denied certiorari by the U.S. Supreme Court thereby allowing a positive ruling by the 9th Circuit Court of Appeals to remain in effect--which resulted in Grethe Cammermeyer, Keith Meinhold, and Mel Dahl all being allowed to serve as openly gay in the service until their retirements as well.

Pruitt was honored for her persistence and courage by many groups during these twelve years, including the cities of Long Beach and Los Angeles, the County of Los Angeles, Lutherans Concerned, MCC, Southern California Women for Understanding, Lambda Legal Defense and Education Fund, and other gay and lesbian organizations. She was named the first *Advocate* Woman of the Year in 1991.

After leaving MCC Long Beach, Pruitt served for five years as the MCC Southwest District's New Works Coordinator and was responsible for six new church starts in that District. She served as pastor of MCC Family in Christ in Fort Collins, Colorado, before retiring from MCC in 2001 with 25 years of service. She is currently an active minister with the United Church of Christ.

In 2006 Pruitt began training for chaplaincy and served as a chaplain resident at Yuma Regional Medical Center, training with Rev. Dr. Earl Cooper, D. Min, and Board-Certified Chaplain. In 2007, she moved to Rehoboth Beach, Delaware, and began Safe Harbor United Church of Christ. In 2013 Safe Harbor became a church in full standing with the Chesapeake Association, Central Atlantic Conference, United Church of Christ. The church meets in Milton, Delaware.

Meantime, Pruitt was hired as a chaplain for Delaware Hospice and served for five years at both the inpatient unit and the home care unit.

In 2009 Dusty was appointed by MCC as Interim Pastor for MCC Rehoboth Beach. She served until 2011 when the church hired a permanent pastor. In 2013, she again was appointed interim pastor and then elected as permanent pastor. She then served as a UCC ordained minister serving an MCC Church. Now, in 2022, she is happily retired.

In 2013 marriage became legal in the state of Delaware. Pruitt married her longtime partner Joanne Rhodes in 2008 when marriage was legal in California prior to Proposition 8 passing. With the end of "Don't Ask, Don't Tell," and the 2013 ruling against the Defense of Marriage Act, Dusty was able to see a lifetime of activism fulfilled. These rulings allowed Dusty to enable her spouse to take part in military and veterans' benefits.

It was in 1985 when Pruitt was pastoring MCC in Long Beach California, she completed and dedicated an old Oddfellows Hall on Pentecost 1985. Shortly after that, she began holding a Charismatic Conference. This became a home for every Spirit-filled believer within MCC as well as many other LGBT believers who were also Spirit-filled but not in MCC. I had heard of it but never made it to one of the dynamic Charismatic Conferences until 1990.

Within the membership of MCC Long beach were two women who had been trained by Youth With A Mission (YWAM) and met on a missions trip in Amsterdam. Sandra Turnbull was an American living in Los Angeles and Janet Robertson was from Scotland. Eventually after that YWAM trip in Europe, their paths crossed again, and they became a couple with Janet moving to the United States. Because they both had a passion for missions, and with the permission of their Pastor, Dusty Pruitt, they made a year's evangelistic ministry trip from May 1988 to May 1989. They traveled around the United States going to whichever of the MCC churches would have them. They sang and preached the Gospel of Jesus Christ. Two other friends from their church, Teri and Ronnie, were also with them.

In the autumn, their little RV broke down in Memphis, TN, so they continued in one vehicle and rode in Teri and Ronnie's camper truck. One of their stops was the MCC in Worchester, MA. It happened to be the same weekend I was also preaching for Rev. Emmitt Watkins there. When I met this traveling troupe, I felt an immediate connection in the Spirit. So, though they were from an MCC and traveling to other MCC churches, I asked if they'd go to a non-MCC church to hold a revival. They happily agreed. They came to Ohio in late November or early December 1988. It was a powerful revival with the four of them. Our folks were blessed, and the bond between us was cemented.

Then they received good news on Christmas Eve from the AAA insurance office in Memphis that the insurance would repair their vehicle after all. They were in New Jersey for the Holidays.

After they returned home in May 1989, they started the first Ministry Training School in the following summer, around July 1990. I was invited to be the first MTS speaker, held at MCC Long Beach under Dr. Dusty Pruitt's pastorate.

When I got to Long Beach, it was also the time Rev. Dusty Pruitt was holding the Charismatic Conference. The School, Encounter Missions International, or EMI, had its classes during the day. The Charismatic Conference services were at night. Rev. Dusty, having never met me, asked to interview me in her office after the classes finished. We visited for about half an hour, and then she invited me to preach one of the services at the Charismatic Conference. I remember preaching from 2 Corinthians 1:20 that the promises of God are "Yes and Amen"!

By day, I was teaching the Baptism of the Holy Spirit and at the end of the sessions, we all went upstairs into the sanctuary. I asked everyone who wanted to receive the Baptism in the Holy Spirit to sit in the front rows. The Spirit instructed me to say that as I laid my hands on them, one by one, they would be filled and begin to speak in tongues. That is exactly what happened. Every single lesbian and gay guy had faith rise in their heart, and they received an infilling of the Holy Spirit and they had their prayer language released.

During my time in Long Beach, I was hosted in a downtown Long Beach hotel. It had a restaurant attached to the lobby. The church instructed me to go there to eat and put the tab on my room bill. I did. One afternoon I went to the restaurant and only a few people were there. I was in a booth, and a lady was in an adjoining booth. In the middle of the room was another man. The waitress came to take my order, and when she did the Holy Spirit spoke to me and said, "Tell her that I have a message for her." This startled me, and I said nothing. She took my order and left. Then great conviction came upon me, and I was feeling like I BETTER obey! On the one hand, I felt like, what if I tell her the Lord has a message for her, and then He doesn't say what it is! I was going to feel like a fool. Also, if I did obey, I was going to be embarrassed in front of all these other (2) customers. I did not want to do this. But on the other hand, if I did not do it, I felt like God was going to kill me at best, or never trust me again at worst!

I surrendered. I repented for not obeying and promised that when she returned, I would tell her that "the Lord had a message for her". Then the waitress disappeared, and it seemed like hours went by while I sweated bullets. Would she ever return? What if she died in the kitchen or something? God was going to kill me; I knew it and her soul was going to be on my hands! If she didn't return soon, I would be having a heart attack and need an ambulance! Finally, (yes FINALLY) she returned. As she set down my beverage, I looked at her and said, THE LORD HAS A MESSAGE FOR YOU! There, I said it! A big weight was lifted. Now I had her attention. She looked at me. The woman in the booth behind me looked at me. The man in the middle of the restaurant looked at me. I looked at God — WHAT NOW? Then BAM! There it was. I said, "when you get home tonight your problem will be solved" She teared up and thanked me. Then the woman in the booth behind me asked, "Did the Lord have a word for her, too?" I declared "NO!" I was glad that was over!

Eventually, Rev. Dusty Pruitt resigned, and ultimately Sandra Turnbull became the pastor of MCC Long Beach. Under her direction, the vision of the church expanded, and EMI began to look at starting churches for the LGBT community along the Pacific Rim. They had a vision for Asia. EMI continued to train students and became a weeklong intensive. It moved from the local church to a college campus for several years. Many people were ministered to and discovered their passion and calling. It didn't take long before a church was started in Taiwan. Janet made several trips to Taiwan and the Lord opened a door for the birthing of a church. Over time, a pastor emerged for this work. Then another pastor emerged, and another work began in Asia. Then, another work began in Australia. There was no stopping this vision of going global with the gospel. Rev. Turnbull still leads this church and this work. Currently, they have transformed into an independent church, with an apostolic mandate. The annual All Nations Gathering now has people from Asia, Australia, Mexico, Europe, and throughout the USA. It is a life-changing event. Her book: *God's Gay Agenda: Gays and Lesbians in the Bible, Church and Marriage* [3] is another one God used to set people free.

The Charismatic Conference continued under Rev. Turnbull's leadership and had a focus on going global with the Gospel. On one occasion, while the church was still MCC of Long Beach, one of the MCC Elders, Rev. Don Eastman was to be a featured speaker. This wasn't too complicated since as an Elder of the denomination he was stationed at the headquarters of MCC in Los Angeles. Long Beach is a short drive down the California coast and would be easy to reach. The worship service began. There were some powerful worship leaders and musicians present. But Elder Don Eastman had not yet arrived. The service continued. And the service continued. And the service continued, but still, no speaker arrived. Finally, when the Spirit began to wind down, and it was time to depart for lunch, then, when the service was basically wrapped up and over, then and only then, did the elder walk into the service. I wondered what Sandy would do. Basically, people had started gathering their things to leave for lunch. But Sandy is a gracious and hospitable leader. She had us all sit down and welcome Elder Rev. Don Eastman.

He stepped up to the podium and was about to start when his phone rang. All eyes were upon him. He stopped everything while he was at the pulpit and took the call. I wondered if God was calling! But it was his office wanting to know if he got there OK. Note to self: don't answer your phone when you're trying to preach.

Rev. Eastman resigned his ministerial credentials with the Assemblies of God and began a new ministry in the lesbian and gay community with Metropolitan Community Churches. He has pastored MCC congregations in Des Moines, Iowa, and Dallas, Texas where he served for 8 ½ years. Under Rev. Eastman's leadership from 1978 to 1986, MCC of Dallas grew to become the largest congregation in the worldwide fellowship. In 1983, Rev. Eastman was elected to the Board of Elders of Metropolitan Community Churches. He was re-elected for five additional terms, serving through 2007. In 1996 Rev. Eastman was listed in *Who's Who in America,* recognizing his role as an activist for the civil and human rights of gays and lesbians.[4] Yes, he had a powerful and pertinent message. But honestly, I can only remember that his phone rang.

Rev. Sandra Turnbull and Tammy Fay

MCC of Long Beach eventually became an independent church called Glory Tabernacle and still hosts the annual conference once called the Charismatic Conference, or more recently called the All Nations Conference. Pastor Sandra Turnbull, the senior pastor, knew in her spirit that Tammy Faye Messner was to be a featured speaker at the evening 6 pm service, Sunday January 25, 2004. There was much spiritual warfare, prayer, and concern about whether Tammy Faye could come or not. She had a medical issue that needed attention and it did not look like she and her husband Roe Messner were coming to California. They called to cancel. Yet, Pastor Turnbull was so certain of hearing from God that she refused to accept anything less than Tammy's full participation in that Sunday service.

By standing in faith, we indeed did see Tammy Faye Messner at the Charismatic Conference in Long Beach California, on Sunday, January 25, 2004, just as God told Pastor Sandra Turnbull. Tammy told us how a history of cancer looked like it was making a comeback. But she got a miracle just prior to coming to California. She also again told the story of Jerry Falwell and the corpse rotting and tied to his back. This was again a media event and well publicized. Glory Tabernacle of Long Beach had an estimated 200 extra people in the service that Sunday night to see Tammy Faye. The net was cast, and many people came to the Lord that night. It was an obvious shift in this move of God.

I realized and shared with others that for a long-time, big-name media personalities in Christianity were holding large crusades all over America, in the largest auditoriums available. But they were not reaping a harvest of unsaved gay folks. Primarily because gay people would not trust them on the Christian turf. But this church in Long Beach was a well-established haven for the gay community. If evangelists wanted to go fishing in the pond of gays, lesbians, transgender, and bisexual folks, they were going to have to come to our pond where the fish could be found. Many came to the Lord and made a commitment to Christ in that haven that night.

In the 1980s Tammy Faye interviewed Rev. Steve Pieters, an AIDS patient on her program, "making an impassioned plea to Christians to love and accept their gay brethren." She was benevolently referred to as "the ultimate drag queen," and said in her last interview with Larry King, "When I went — when we lost everything, it was the gay people that came to my rescue, and I will always love them for that." On July 20, 2007, Messner died at her home in Loch Lloyd, near Kansas City, Missouri, after an eleven-year bout with cancer. She was 65 years old. A family service was held on the morning of July 21, at the Messner family plot in Waldron, Kansas. The ceremony was officiated by Rev. Randy McCain, the pastor of the affirming Open Door Community Church in Sherwood, Arkansas.[5]

Rev. Randy McCain, who is another gay pastor in this LGBT-affirming move of God, befriended Tammy in her final years.[6]

143

[1] http://dustypruitt.com/?page_id=50 last accessed October 17, 2015

[2] http://dustypruitt.com/?page_id=33 last accessed October 17, 2015

[3] Turnbull, Sandra, *God's Gay Agenda: Gays and Lesbians in the Bible, Church, and Marriage*, Glory Press, Long Beach CA 2012

[4] http://www.lgbtran.org/Profile.aspx?ID=258 last accessed October 17, 2015

[5] Tammy Faye Messner - Wikipedia (last accessed 7/6/2022)

[6] Rev. Randy McCain is the author of the book: *And God Save Judy Garland: A gay Christian's journey*, Prescient Books, 2014

Heterosexuals who Moved Toward US

Sylvia Pennington

Sylvia Pennington was the most famous early forerunner.

An Assemblies of God Minister, Sylvia went to San Francisco to convert gays in the 1970s.

The Rev. Sylvia Pennington was an early pioneer in the Christian LGBT community as an ordained heterosexual woman sharing God's all-inclusive love with "Whosoevers" all over the world.

Sylvia began life in a Scottish Orthodox Jewish family with two older sisters who were very much a part of her life and ministry. She married and had a son. When her husband took his own life, she was left alone with her son. Her sisters and mom had moved to California. She began her journey with Jesus through an encounter with the Holy Spirit at a church in the Ozark Mountains of Arkansas on her way to California. This relationship with Jesus began in the early 1960s and led her to an Assemblies of God church in Los Angeles. There she heard about a ministry to homosexuals in San Francisco. Sylvia and her friend Ruth felt they were called to go "change" the gays to be straight. However, she was torn because she really loved Jesus but was also falling in love with Harry Pennington. Deciding she had to put some distance between herself and Harry, Sylvia went with Ruth to San Francisco to Glad Tidings Church. There they brought a lot of gay/lesbian people to church. Harry followed them to San Francisco and Sylvia and Harry were married. After three months there, they went back home to the Los Angeles area. Later, while on another trip to San Francisco, Sylvia noticed that none of the "former gays" were still in the church. She was concerned and decided to go to their homes and look them up. She listened to peoples' stories and heard that they had tried to be what the church wanted them to be, but that they hadn't "changed." Sylvia began to see that being gay wasn't any different from being heterosexual; one just loved someone of the same gender.

She went back home to Los Angeles to think this over. Sylvia's friend Ruth wrote the foreword to *But Lord, They're Gay* and said this about Sylvia: "There are a great many that can say they have come to know God in a deeper way through His love manifest in her." A gay man, Bob, whom Sylvia had met in San Francisco called and wanted to stay with her on his trip to Los Angeles. He invited her to the Metropolitan Community Church (MCC). Covering herself with much prayer, she went to the church and was surprised to find God's gay/lesbian/transgender people there loving God and moved by the Holy Spirit. She asked and questioned: "God, how could this be?" Sylvia knew what she had witnessed that night and from there began what she described as her "changing years" that eventually led her to pastor in MCCs and to minister all over the U.S. and Canada: preaching, counseling, leading workshops, writing three books, and always sharing God's all-inclusive love with everyone. The Rev. Sylvia Pennington became an ordained heterosexual minister in the Universal Fellowship of Metropolitan Community Churches. After her license was not renewed, the church she was pastoring withdrew from the Fellowship and she continued pastoring for a time with Lambda Christian Fellowship in Hawthorne, California. She continued ministry under the name of Lambda Christian Fellowship until her untimely death. Sylvia's first book, *But Lord, They're Gay* is both her story and the story of five Christian gay/lesbian people telling their stories about growing up Christian and gay/lesbian. The second book was a response to the growing biblical attacks against gay people in 1985 and was one of the first books written about the scriptural passages used to condemn GLBT peoples, *Good News For Modern Gays: A*

Pro-Gay Biblical Approach. Then in 1989, she published her last book, *Ex-Gays: There Are None!*, from interviews she had done with more than a dozen people over the years, learning that many had tried not to be LGBT by going through change ministries, marriage, careers, ministry, and other ways only to find that they are still God's LGBT daughters and sons. Sylvia received hundreds of letters from people all over the world and replied to every one of them. She often called people after receiving a letter and the other person would begin crying in unbelief that she would reach out this way and care about them... Sylvia died young at 60 on April 13, 1991, due to complications from congestive heart failure and diabetes.[1]

Evelyn and Dennis Schave

Rev. Evelyn and Dennis Schave

Evelyn and her husband Dennis Schave pastored a church in Centralia, Washington. They began to pray that the Lord would send into their church anyone that God wanted to be there. Many years before this, when Evelyn was single, she and another woman, Naomi Harvey, traveled America as singing and preaching evangelists. It never occurred to Evelyn that Naomi was a lesbian. Naomi was a preacher and gospel singer. In Evelyn's mind, that wasn't compatible with also being gay. When they got off the road, they opened a drug rehabilitation center and church. Dennis Schave became one of the clients. He and Evelyn got married, and that left no more room for Naomi.

Naomi was in a lesbian relationship, though at the time, Evelyn was not aware this was the case. The woman left Naomi for another woman, then said she wanted to come back to her. Naomi went to pick up her lover and bring her home when she got into an altercation with the new lover. As the two women argued, Naomi grabbed a gun out of her car and killed the competitor as this woman sat at the wheel of her own car. In 1980 her life was changed by a second-degree murder sentence that sent her to prison for 17 years to life. She served five years before her sentence was vacated by the 5th appellate court in California because of Diminished capacity at the time of the crime.[2] When Naomi was arrested, Evelyn was convinced, that because of the lesbian affair, "God had given her up to a reprobate mind."

While in prison, Naomi had an angelic visitation and was told that God was bringing her out of prison. Soon after this, she was released. While Evelyn and Dennis were praying for God to send in whoever He wanted, one day Naomi came with a new lover on her arm. The church in that small town knew who Naomi was and her history. They demanded to know what Pastor Dennis and Evelyn were going to do about this! Of course, they expected them to cast Naomi and her woman into the outer darkness!

But Evelyn and Dennis remembered that this was their prayer-whoever God wanted was welcome. They held their ground and said Naomi was welcome. The church vehemently disagreed. The board resigned. The members left. Evelyn and Dennis were left with an empty building. People threw eggs at the church building, and others dumped garbage in the parking lot. The church closed.

In the meantime, the anointing on Naomi had not left. She started two LGBT-affirming churches. One was in Portland, Oregon, and one in Seattle, Washington. She invited Evelyn to come and see what God was doing. She did go to a service but was very skeptical. She was sure God couldn't love gay people unless they repented of their homosexuality. This, she felt, was a travesty. Simultaneously, Naomi had been on the board of Advance Christian Ministries, which hosted the Advance Conferences in Texas. She asked Evelyn if she'd be willing to come along and see what God was doing. She wasn't too keen on the idea, but when Naomi told Tom Hirsch she was bringing Evelyn along, Tom asked Evelyn if she would preach.

Evelyn was now in a quandary. What should she do? She asked other minister friends. They said — YES! They'd love to preach to a whole room of homosexual sinners and get them saved! She asked Dennis what she should do. He reminded her that she always said she'd go preach wherever a door was open. She accepted. She was certain that God was going to have her preach repentance and salvation to these homosexuals. In 1989 Evelyn was flown into Dallas for the Advance Conference. She didn't just walk in and preach and leave. She was there for the whole conference and though she was the first speaker, worship and prayer happened first. She watched and studied. She said she was there as a "Looky Loo".

Worship began that first October night. It was real, heartfelt worship. Jesus was being magnified, the Holy Spirit hovered, Angels were present, and all Evelyn could do was weep. She testified that as a Christian for many years, she knew the presence of the Holy Spirit, and He was certainly right there, with these gay people!

Then it was time for her to preach. She just began to minister about the love of God. People came forward for prayer. People were receiving the baptism in the Holy Spirit, speaking in tongues, getting slain in the Spirit, getting healed of various things, and being set free. But she saw that God was not changing anyone's sexual orientation. Not then, not ever! Not anymore than God changes people's eye color. She got it! She called Dennis and all she could do was cry. Dennis later said that here his wife was calling him long distance and ran up the phone bill saying nothing, just crying. Those were tears of joy and amazement at what God was doing.

This was Evelyn's first real encounter with the Holy Spirit and gay people. It was her eye-opening revelation. She told Dennis he just had to also come the next year to see for himself. During that conference, I was having some trouble back home in our church and needed some wise counsel. I figured Evelyn had been in ministry more than any of us, and I felt I could trust her. At lunch the next day we sat together, and I poured out my heart. She gave me sound advice, and it was then that I trusted her. I asked if she'd come to preach at our church in Dayton, Ohio. She agreed.

The date was set, as a weekend in March 1990. What I didn't know was that this was the first gay church she was going to preach in. I am not sure I would have been so eager for her to come if I knew that.

She had lots of questions after that Advance conference. When she got home, she wanted to know how God was doing this with gays; was there a separate standard for gays than for straights, and what happened after we got saved? What about the Bible? There were lots of questions. She asked Naomi all these things, but she said, "You're going to Samuel Kader's church. He's the one to ask your questions.

March 1990 came. It was the last weekend in March and was also Evelyn's birthday. She didn't know that I knew this. We had a marvelous weekend revival. The Holy Spirit moved, and people got healed and touched by God. Everyone present heard from God that weekend. But when the revival was over, we went home from the Sunday morning service. Evelyn, who only preached in dresses and high heels, asked if we would be offended if she got comfortable and wore slacks. What was the big deal? All my lesbians only wore slacks. She was the only one in a dress. Of course, from her holiness background, this is all women should wear. No church people should ever see her without wearing a dress.

I said, "Sure, go ahead."

What she didn't know was that I had invited the whole church to come over to celebrate her birthday, as a surprise. When they came over, she was horrified! She was an old-timey Pentecostal preacher and would never, ever, let church people see her in slacks! We all thought that was so funny! Our lesbians would never let anyone see them in a dress! She learned there were some traditions she too could be freed from. But for the next thirty years, she still preached in a dress. That gave gay guys a great opportunity to dress up Miss Evelyn. They bought her scarves, heels, broaches, jewelry, dresses, and matching hankies of only the fanciest kind. She was a living drag queen's dream! Her clothes and shoes either made gay men jealous or inspired them. She always looked *fabulous*!

Evelyn has a habit of pacing up and down an aisle when she preaches. In the process, she usually smacks people who sit on the aisle as she makes her points. Eventually, that became a trademark and people would make a point of sitting on the aisle, so they'd get smacked by Miss Evelyn.

After the birthday party wound down, and our folks headed home, Evelyn said she'd like to ask me a few questions. The most important to settle for her was whether there was a separate holiness standard for gay people in their relationships as for straights. I told her no; God is no respecter of persons. (Remember, that was something I had to learn). The same expectation of love and respect and faithfulness in a marriage between a man and woman was also the standard for gay couples. She was surprised at that, but also pleased to hear it. It let her relax, knowing she wasn't going to offend us if she made some reference to these standards. Then later that night, when we all settled in for bed, the Lord told her that if she had questions to ask Him directly. He'd show her the answers. She and Dennis were from that point on being called to the LGBT community. And as preachers, teachers, and evangelists, they were also known as Mom and Pop.

The next year, 1991, when I had Evelyn back to preach, I was getting ready for the Sunday morning service. I was setting up communion, pulling the songs for the overhead projector, (yes that's what we had back then), and a hundred other things. Evelyn, my spouse Robert, and a heterosexual member of the church named Dave Fritts were all in the sanctuary hanging out. I felt very distracted like I was running out of time. I was getting frazzled. In the meantime, like a caged tiger, Evelyn kept pacing up and down the aisle saying, "We have got to pray, we have got to pray." I was getting annoyed because I felt like who had time to pray? I was like Martha in the Mary and Martha parable. "Lord, don't you care that I have to do all this by myself?" So finally, exasperated, I said, "Alright! Let's pray then!" I didn't say it in a very charitable manner. We gathered together in a circle, Evelyn, Robert, Dave Fritts, and me. We held hands and began praying in the Spirit, in tongues.

Then it dawned on me that Dave Fritts was praying in tongues!! I was his pastor. He never told me he had the baptism of the Holy Spirit. Why didn't he ever tell me this? Now I was really offended! So as soon as we were finished praying, I said, "Dave, I want to see you in my office!" He came in and I asked him, "Dave, when did you get the baptism in the Holy Spirit and speak in tongues?"

He answered, "Just then as we were praying." It had just happened as we prayed. No wonder Evelyn kept saying, "We have got to pray, we have got to pray."

OK, God, you win. I get it.

On another occasion, in May 1994, I had Evelyn as my guest speaker, but there was a singing duo out of MCC New York, called David and Jane. David was a teacher at Julliard in New York, and Jane taught music in the New Your City school district. Imagine with all the talent in New York how good you'd have to be to teach music there. They were remarkable. But inviting them to sing caused me to learn a valuable lesson. The revival with Evelyn was scheduled for Thursday, May 19, Friday, Saturday, and Sunday. But since David and Jane both worked, they could not fly out of New York until Thursday afternoon. They were to sing on Thursday and Friday nights. May in Ohio can be tricky, and it was snowing. That kept their plane on the ground in New York. It was time for the service to begin, and they had not yet landed in Dayton.

Evelyn not only preaches, but she could play piano as well. In the midst of the service, I got the phone call that their plane had landed. Now I had to leave the service and go to the Dayton airport to pick up

David and Jane. I left Evelyn in charge to carry on. Evelyn is a trouper. She just went ahead and carried the service until we returned. It was a twenty-minute drive to the airport in each direction. When we arrived back, we had David and Jane sing immediately. The lesson learned was to never again trust the airlines to get someone to a church service the same day. From that day on I brought in speakers on the day before.

After she preached at our church, Evelyn became quite a popular preacher in our affirming churches and at our LGBT-affirming conferences. She and Dennis were on the go continuously. They were touching many lives for God, and the word was out. After they had been ministering to gay people for several years, they were invited to be guest speakers at the Charismatic Conference hosted by Rev. Sandy Turnbull, in Long Beach, California. Jerry and I also attended.

Two other surprise guest speakers were famous Country Gospel Singers Dony McGuire and his wife Reba Rambo. Dony was one of Christian music's most beloved and sought-after artists. His wife Reba was equally famous. Who expected this caliber of ministers to visit us? The move of God was also reaching other heterosexual Christians who were listening to what God was saying and doing. Rev. Turnbull had invited them to speak as well. But when it was Rev. Dony McGuire's time to speak, he acknowledged the price Evelyn and Dennis had paid to pave the way and be vanguards in this movement. He asked them to come on stage, as well as the other pastors present. Then he and Reba removed their shoes and socks and washed their feet. This was a tear-invoking, overwhelming, emotional night in the presence of a Holy God. Dony and Reba honored them as pioneers and also repented for the years that they wronged the gay community.

Dennis and Evelyn continue to minister as the Holy Spirit leads. They are truly pioneers. But part of this can be explained by the prayer Evelyn prayed as a young evangelist. She always said, "God, whatever you're doing, I don't want to be left out! I want to be in the big middle of any move you have!" God has honored that prayer. Currently, they attend church at Doug Clanton's RPI church in Phoenix Arizona.

Doris Swartz. / Betty Hill

Betty Hill — Go boldly into the Body of Christ

I used to also attend a local Pentecostal church in Dayton, Ohio, as well as pastor my own. Our service was only in the morning and a few blocks from my house was an independent Pentecostal church pastored by a minister named Doris Swartz. They had a Sunday evening service at 6 pm and I enjoyed going there to see what God might have to say. She often had prophets and evangelists as guest speakers, and I enjoyed of the wealth of wisdom coming from within the Body of Christ. One day she had a prophet named Betty Hill preach. Normally I kept a low profile in that church, so I wouldn't cause controversy, I knew the majority of Pentecostal churches were opposed to homosexuality, and I wasn't there to raise a gay pride flag. I just was hungry for more of God. I sat in the back and left as soon as service was over. That's why I was surprised when Betty Hill called me forward to speak a word over me. Without knowing me or to whom I ministered, she said I had a ministry that the rest of the Body needed; and for me to Go Boldly into the Body of Christ.

I know she was unaware that my ministry was primarily to gays and lesbians, but she said to go boldly, nonetheless. That seemed empowering. But then on occasion Pastor Doris would have one of those preachers who felt the need to speak against their concept of the "gay agenda" and there I'd be, feeling pretty put off. After one more of those preachers carried on about this, I got fed up and left. Politely of course, but left, nevertheless. I decided I had enough of the homophobia preached from America's pulpits and was not going to return to Doris Swartz's church.

God had other plans. It seemed everywhere I went, whether the post office, the grocery store or anywhere else, I'd run into people from her church. I'd try to avoid them, but they'd always see me and tell me how much they missed seeing me. Then came the big one! Our church had gone out to eat after our morning service, and so had hers. We ended up at the same Chinese buffet together, and it wasn't a very big place. I was cordial and said hello, but then Pastor Doris made a point of coming over to me and asking a very pointed question. She asked if she had offended me in some way. Well, it wasn't her personally, it was those other guest speakers who felt they had to correct America's homosexual problem. So, it wasn't her directly, so I said no. I still had no intention of returning, however.

I wasn't being completely truthful, and God dealt with me. So, the next day on Monday, I called her up and asked if I could come to see her in her office. She was available right then. When I entered her office, I told her I wanted her to know why I left her church. I started off by telling her that not only was I gay, but that almost all the people in my church were as well. I explained that my primary ministry was to the gay-affirming community.

Doris shocked me. She said, "I know that."

WHAT!? She did?

She said as soon as I came to visit her church the very first time, she knew I was gay. Now I didn't think I was that flaming obvious, but she said she knew by the Spirit. But, she said, "I also found you in the Spirit, and I know you're not promiscuous". She said I was welcome there, and if I had a Word from God to preach, I was welcome to share it. She also understood how sometimes her pulpit could be used by others to say some pretty offensive things. She said she didn't think she could control that. She was the president of an international fellowship of Pentecostal ministers and churches, and once a year they had an annual conference at her church. (International Ministers' Forum)

I asked, "Well, what if her people found out about my ministry, and wanted to call her on the carpet about it?"

She said she'd tell them that she is not responsible for another man's ministry.

But she had another thing to say. She remembered that I said my ministry was primarily to the gay community. She said don't limit yourself. She said if you say you're a minister to the gay community primarily, that's all you have and all you'll be known for. Instead, be open to ministering to whomever God sends in. That changed my focus.

Occasionally, when our church had Rev. Thomas Hirsch preach for us, I took Tom with me to Doris's evening church service. After our revival at our church had ended, she called me up and asked me to come over to her house. She told me that she remembered who Thomas was. In his earlier days, Tom was the worship leader for another Pentecostal church in Buffalo NY. Sister Doris was best friends with his pastor, Rev. Mary. They were all in the same International Ministers' Forum. Someone from Sister Mary's church saw Thomas hanging out in a known notorious homosexual hangout area. (Why the informer was there wasn't considered). Once they suspected that Tom was gay, he was called on the carpet, and he did not deny his homosexuality. He was rejected and cast out of the church. As a result, Thomas Hirsch moved to Dallas, Texas. He would often testify that if he was going to hell, he was going to make it worth his while. So, he said, he led a wild life for a time. But God wouldn't let him go, and over time called him to begin his own church, Circle of Glory. Doris told me privately that she knew what she heard about him in Buffalo but wasn't making any judgments about it. He was still welcome to visit her church when in town. Pastor Doris Swartz was the epitome of grace.

Interestingly enough, it was in this church, during one of those powerfully anointed conferences she hosted, that the Holy Spirit told me for the second time that I was not a general. I was having issues with Thomas Hirsch and his leadership style and considering leaving the Advance Conference he led. But when the Spirit of God became so heavy in Doris's church, I fell on my face in His presence. It was then God said I was not a general, and thus He wanted me to remain in the Alliance of Christian Churches and still attend the Advance conference under Thomas Hirsch's leadership, despite my opinion about it. It's hard to argue with God; one of us is going to win the argument, and it has yet to be me.

In 1999 my book was published, *Openly Gay, Openly Christian, How the Bible Really is Gay Friendly*.[3] The local newspaper, *The Dayton Daily News* ran a half-page story about it, including a picture of me holding my book. I thought, well, this will be the end of me going to Pastor Doris' United Christian Center. But I was wrong. Instead, several members of her congregation called our church to leave me a message. One, in particular, was from a woman I had come to love as a Christian sister, who, in her message said she apologized. She said in all the 13 years I had been going there, she never knew my last name. She apologized for this ignorance on her part. There was no negativity on their part whatsoever. Then, Pastor Doris's son, David Swartz, asked how he could get a copy of my book. He admitted that he would run into gay men from time to time and just didn't know how to minister to them. Suddenly a door opened into the hearts and minds of my sisters and brothers because they knew a real live person, not a concept. And they already loved me; just like Jesus told them to.

[1] http://www.lgbtran.org/Profile.aspx?ID=131 last accessed October 17, 2015

[2]   https://www.facebook.com/revnaomi/about?section=bio&lst= 1392073104%3A1380379505%3A1583006797   (last   accessed 2-29-2020)

[3] Kader, Rev. Samuel, *Openly Gay, Openly Christian, How the Bible Really is Gay Friendly*, Leyland Press, San Francisco, 1999, revised 2013

The Prophecies

Benny Hinn

Bill Roberts, my co-pastor at Community Gospel Church in Dayton Ohio called me one day and asked if I saw the *Praise the Lord* program on the Trinity Broadcasting Network the night before. I said no. He said, well, it had been on at 11 pm the night before, and was going to be rebroadcast today at 5 pm. I should come over to his house and see what the famous evangelist Benny Hinn said about gay people on the program. I didn't have a television, so I walked the two blocks to his house to see the rebroadcast. Bill had a tape recorder ready to copy every word that was said. He also typed it up and I sent a transcript of it to Benny Hinn's offices the next day. I got a very nice letter from Hinn's secretary thanking me for the typed transcript. I sent it to Benny Hinn to confirm that this is what Hinn actually said. They never denied his words.

On February 28, 1989, Evangelist Benny Hinn was on the *Praise the Lord* program on the Trinity Broadcasting Network. He was being interviewed by the host Paul Crouch. I watched the program, and they were talking about the next great wave of God, and how it would happen. Over and over Hinn said he was praying about this, and he saw a vision of a tidal wave (which represented revival, he explained) hitting the whole earth, coming from outer space. But this move of God was not going to start in the large churches of America but in small groups. And it would be spearheaded by those whom he personally considered a plagued people. Paul Crouch asked Hinn who that might be.

Hinn seemed very uncomfortable to admit this, but then clearly said it was *the homosexuals*.

Hinn said those churches which would embrace gays would be in the next tidal wave of what God was going to do. Hinn said he told God, "But I don't want any plagued people coming into my church! I'm comfortable with what I have."

Hinn reported that God asked him a question:

"Do you believe I can do this?" Hinn slowly answered "Yes". He saw that in the 1970's the unappreciated and undesired people were the Hippies. Those churches that opened their arms to them flourished. This would be the same. Hinn reported that God declared that God was going to prove to the church and to the world that He could clean them up.

What was interesting was the audience's reaction to this declaration. At first, there was a long silence. Then as people filtered what Hinn had said through their religious mindset, they made the assumption that God was going to convert homosexuals into non-gays. Then applause broke out. But God had stated [1] to Hinn that He was going to prove to the world and to the church that He was going to clean gays up. That is exactly what God has been doing. It is for this reason that gay people even had the vision to be married and have stable loving same-sex relationships. The former ways of promiscuity have fallen out of favor among those who love God and want to follow His ways.

God told Peter that what He had cleansed to not call unclean! He told Hinn the same thing. Benny Hinn said that God will prove to the world and to the Church that He can clean them [gays] up. That's exactly what God is doing. We used to be a people of the night, walking in shadows and ashamed to say our names. But God has given us a name that is better than that of sons and daughters; the promise to the eunuchs of Isaiah 56: 3-6 is transpiring before our very eyes in one generation since 1968.

Simon Le Vay [2] 29 January 1991; accepted 24 June 1991.

In January of 1991, in my prayer time, the Holy Spirit said to me that: "By your Birthday I am going to prove to the world you are born this way"

My birthday is in September. Suddenly in June, I came across an article about the discovery that neuroscientist Simon LeVay, a former Harvard University researcher, had made. He evaluated the brains of gay men vs the brains of straight men during autopsy. He found a distinct difference in the hypothalamus.

In 1991 LeVay published a controversial paper in the journal Science that described an anatomical difference between the brains of homosexual and heterosexual men. Specifically, he found that a structure called the third interstitial nucleus of the anterior hypothalamus (INAH-3) was smaller in the brains of gay men than it was in men known or assumed to be heterosexual.

In his seminar, LeVay described his own work and that of other researchers who give nature their vote in the nature versus nurture debate. LeVay referred to studies of separately raised twins that suggest that sexual orientation has a genetic component. LeVay went on to describe a 1993 study by Dean H. Hamer of the National Cancer Institute. The two have collaborated on writing about their field for the general public. In his study of 40 pairs of gay brothers, Hamer's group found a specific region of the X chromosome seemed to be associated with homosexuality. [3]

Immediately after this information was released the religious right began their attack to discredit anything LeVay might have to offer. But he was only proving what any gay person already knew; we didn't choose to be gay; we were born this way. But now the Holy Spirit even prophesied to me that He was going to bring this proof forward; and that it would happen before my birthday in September of 1991.

Subsequently there have been so many articles about gay animals: rams, cattle, horses, penguins, dogs, cats, sheep, swans, and even fruit flies (no pun intended), showing that homosexual love is common in nature as well as people.[4]

It was widely reported back in 1967 that one of Canada's last royal swans was mourned by his same-sex partner. There were twelve swans donated to Ottawa by the Queen in 1967 and one has died, leaving behind his crestfallen male mate. Patch, a white swan who lost an eye ten years prior, was found dead ...Now the keepers in charge of the royal swan collection say that if they look for a new partner for Buddy, Patch's life partner, they will try to accommodate his same-sex preference. "It happens in the wild from time to time," Christine Hartig, the city employee in charge of the swans, said of the male pairing. "They'd been together for years. We never dreamt of separating them." The two swans stuck together in their own section of the Rideau River and shared a pen in the swan collection's custom-built wintering facilities. They would often be seen grooming each other and engaging in customary swan mating rituals... Now that Patch has died, Ms. Hartig said, that Buddy would probably need a new mate. "If it was a gay couple, so what? The purpose was not to reproduce," she said. She added that ... "If I can find him a male, I will," she said. Then as the story unfolded, Buddy had moved on to a much younger male swan by the next season.[5]

Undercover Prophesies

I realized that God is preparing His church, little by little to understand that things He's doing are outside of their religious box. But God is like that! In John 10 Jesus announces to His disciples that He has "Other sheep, which are not of this fold, and these He must also bring in" He was saying this to His first-century Jewish disciples. Since that time, He brought in Samaritans, Roman soldiers, and Gentiles of every kind. He brought women to the forefront as leaders and pastors of churches, and now He has been moving among gay people, bisexuals, trans folks, and others still.

A heterosexual couple in my church has been also attending prophetic sessions held by another church. The church is not affirming, but they do flow in the Spirit. Mr. and Mrs. Yake went forward for a prophecy and the pastor told them that their ministry is outside the box. Yes, that's true. That minister would have no idea that the church they attend has gay pastors, nor would they approve of it. But God is doing this work nonetheless, without asking for their approval. While the conservative religious people in the Body try hard to get legislators elected who will oppose LGBT-friendly laws and legislation, they are on the wrong side of history. God keeps marching forward drawing His Others to Himself.

But one day the Body must be without spot or wrinkle. The divisions in the Body and the walls erected must come down. God is doing this gently. They see that God is moving among people who are wired differently or working outside the box. Yes, that's exactly what God is doing.

And God has been trying to tell His kids this news for quite a while.

[1] Benny Hinn, *Praise The Lord Program* Trinity Broadcasting Live, Trinity Broadcasting Network [TBN] 2/28/1989 11 p.m. EST.

[2] A summary of LeVay's work can be read at: http://www-2.cs.cmu.edu/afs/cs.cmu.edu/user/scotts/bulgarians/nature-nurture/levay.html

[3] LeVay Shares Thoughts On 'Gay Gene' Research — The Tech (mit. edu) http://tech.mit.edu/V116/N27/levay.27n. html (last accessed 7/8/2022)

[4] Just google "homosexual behavior in animals" in my many years of studying this topic I have more articles than could ever be referenced.

[5] https://schetenei.livejournal.com/16426.html (last accessed July 8, 2022

Case Studies in Scripture

Though my last book, *Openly Gay, Openly Christian, How the Bible Really is Gay Friendly*, already goes deeply into the original meaning of the Scriptural passages that are used to condemn gay people, I feel a quick review is still appropriate here.

ROMANS 1

Many times, if a Bible has a concordance at the back, and if among the topics listed is the topic of homosexuality, then usually Romans chapter one will be the reference cited, particularly verses 26-27. Romans 1:26 is the only verse in the whole Bible that deals with women being sexually active with women. There is no other such verse anywhere.

It is important to also note that the Bible says that out of the mouth of *two or three witnesses* let every word be established [1].

Therefore, to make a case about lesbianism in the Word of God, there should be *at least* one other scripture to deal with the topic of women being sexually involved with other women. But there isn't.

There are other topics in the Bible as well, about which conclusive doctrines cannot be built. This is because these topics are merely mentioned once. Paul makes only one passing reference to baptism for the dead, and that is to the Corinthians [2]. We don't know what he was talking about in that situation, and his one reference is not enough information upon which to build a solid doctrine about the issue.

Yet this is the only reference in the entire word of God that talks about women being with women. The footnotes, end notes, and marginal notes within various Bibles are not the inspired word of God. When a concordance lists the topic of homosexuality and then cites Romans 1:26-27, that footnote is not God-breathed. A footnote is someone's opinion, or further explanation but not God's.

When you study the Bible, you need to ask yourself some questions in order to understand what the Bible is saying. You can't take scripture out of context and arrive at its truth. Yet if I were to tell people who knew little or nothing about the Bible that the Bible says Judas went and hung himself, and Jesus says in the Bible to go and do likewise, therefore the Bible condones suicide by hanging, it is obvious I am twisting the scriptures by taking them out of context. What I do in such a case is actually an abortion to the intent and truth of the Word, even though I am quoting the truly recorded words of the Bible. Yet this process is exactly what occurs when people try to make Romans 1:26-27 a condemnation of homosexuality.

When a scripture verse begins with *therefore* it is important to know for what purpose it is there. It is obviously connected in thought to the previous verses. When the word *therefore* or a similar type of connective word is used to start a verse, it is important to see what came before this verse, since it is obviously attached in thought, content, and context to the previous thought. It is there to build a case, and it is important to see why they are using the connective word. We need to ask ourselves "What is the point the writer is trying to make?" We need to know. The verse needs its context. This is important to understand in any kind of Bible exegesis. And it is especially true here in Romans chapter one.

We will start by taking these two verses out of context to see what they say when they stand alone and see why people say these verses are against homosexuals, and then try to make their case that God hates homosexuals.

Rom 1:26-27

26 *Because of this*, God gave them over to shameful lusts. Even their women exchanged natural relations for unnatural ones.

27 In the same way, the men also abandoned natural relations with women and were inflamed with lust for one another. Men committed indecent acts with other men and received in themselves the due penalty for their perversion. (NIV)

Note that in spite of the Bible version being read, verse 26 starts out by saying something similar to, *therefore*, or another word that means "because of what you just read...". NIV states "Because of this...." you can't read those three words without asking, Because of *what*? These verses are also attached to the verses before them and the verses after. The next verse, verse 28, begins with the word *and*, which also means there is more than what we've just read.

We can see there is more than an isolated scripture here, so we ask to whom is Paul writing to? He is writing to the first-century Christian church at Rome. He is not writing to an organized church for and by gays in metropolitan ancient Rome. He is not writing to gay people at all. He is writing to an audience that is both heterosexual and Christian.

This verse 26, written to the heterosexual church in Rome says: "Because of this [we still need to see because of *what*] God gave them up unto vile affections: for even their women did *change* [or *exchange*] the natural use...".

The word *change* is # 3337 in *Strong's* [3]. It means to *exchange*. What does exchange mean? It means I have to have something that I will let go of in order to trade it for something else. If I have a shirt, and I take it back to the store to *exchange* it, I have to have an original shirt in the beginning in order to trade, or exchange, for a different shirt. But in order to *exchange* anything, I have to have something initially.

These women exchanged the *natural* use. The word *natural* is # 5546 in *Strong's* [4]. It means *instinctive*. What they are exchanging is their instinctive use. In other words, a heterosexual woman has the basic instincts to have sexual relationships with a heterosexual man. These are her instincts. As a little girl perhaps she thinks about boyfriends, having a husband, playing house, and playing mommy. You look at her childhood to see what instincts she has and see what is ingrained in her. If a non- heterosexual woman is going to *exchange* what is natural or *instinctive* to her, it means she would have to exchange what is natural to her, what is instinctive in her, what is not natural to her, and what is not instinctive in her. These women did exchange the natural use for that which is against their own nature, as heterosexuals. They exchanged their heterosexual *orientation* for homosexual *activity*. Not for a homosexual orientation, because a heterosexual person cannot make themselves have a different orientation, but they could pick up a different behavior that is not instinctive to them. They exchanged their orientation for certain sexual behavior.

The next verse says, "and likewise also the men...." This tells us that whatever we can infer about the women, we can likewise infer about the men. It is likewise, or the same way for the men as for the women. Likewise, the men leaving the *natural* use... Again, it's the same word, *natural* or *instinctive*, meaning their own instincts as heterosexuals. They left their own instinctive use of the woman. Which man would have an *instinctive* use of a woman, a *heterosexual* man or a *homosexual* man? A heterosexual man. He has a natural instinctive use of a woman.

He *leaves* that. To *leave* is # 863 in *Strong's* [5], means *having forsaken*, to *send away*, to *lay aside* the instinctive use, to *leave* their natural use, or to *yield up* their natural use of the woman.

They *burned* in their lust. To *burn* is #1572 in *Strong's* [6], and it means to *inflame deeply*. If you look in *Strong's* or *New Englishman's* [7], you discover there are other Greek words for burn, but the difference in this word is that it has a prefix which shows that is more than a simple burning, it is an all-consuming burning; it burns deeply. The person is consumed with this lust. It is a deeply burning inflammation of lust. It is lust at the point of orgasm where there is no turning back. At that point, it doesn't matter what consequences follow.

They are burning in *lust*. The word lust is interesting. It is a consuming craving and lust as we might expect the word to say. It is # 3715 in

Strong's [8], meaning lust, excitement of the mind, longing after, craving. What the Bible does not say is also interesting. It does not say they are burning in their *love* for one another. It is pure raw sexual lust for the sake of sex alone.

What does that have to do with a gay male or lesbian couple who love each other and have made the commitment to love, honor, and cherish one another until death do they part? Nothing. They are unrelated topics. In a gay coupled relationship neither partner has *exchanged* their natural instinct for anything else. They have not given up what is instinctive or natural to them.

There are questions to ask from just these verses without even looking at the surrounding text. We ask is a person who is in a same-sex relationship leaving what is *natural* and *instinctive* for them? We also ask are they burning in *lust* or are they walking in *love*? God is love. Love comes from God. God is the source of love. When people condemn a gay relationship as if it was wrong and immoral and declare God hates it and that God will condemn it; shows a lack of understanding of the source of love. You have to ask yourself is this a *lustful* relationship? In a lustful relationship, the only thing that matters is sex. If you're inflamed and burning in lust, the only thing that matters is sexual pressure being relieved. You couldn't care less about the other person. That kind of event occurs all the time. People do get arrested or fined for public sexual activity.

In a prison setting, people who might have a heterosexual orientation will exchange that natural orientation for a temporary lapse into a lustful sexual liaison for the sake of sex alone. Once released from prison, they don't pursue same-sex encounters.

Without even digging further or studying the two verses in their context we see the issue is *lust*, not *love*. The cause of this lustful behavior is listed in the chapter. After we really look at this passage, we begin to see whom God is talking about, and how they got to the place where they are having raw, lustful homosexual *activity*. We will need to go back a few verses in Romans 1 to see the whole story.

Romans 1 begins with Paul addressing the Church. He gives a greeting to the church in the Name of the Lord and identifies who is writing. He states why he is writing, and how he is not ashamed of the Gospel of Christ. He establishes that the righteous live by faith. Then we pick up verse 18.

Rom 1:18

18 The wrath of God is being revealed from heaven against all the godlessness and wickedness of men who suppress the truth by their wickedness,

Paul begins to address ungodliness; he is talking about people walking in *all ungodliness* and *all unrighteousness* of mortals, [*men # 444 in Strong's Anthropos: mortals, humans; male and female.*]. He is addressing people who do not walk in a godly way.

Rom 1:19

19 since what may be known about God is plain to them, because God has made it plain to them.

So far, we see these people walking in *all* ungodliness and *all* unrighteousness, in spite of the fact God has shown them what is right.

This scripture goes on to declare:

Rom 1:20

20 For since the creation of the world God's invisible qualities-- his eternal power and divine nature-- have been clearly seen, being understood from what has been made, *so that men are without excuse.*

Paul is talking about people who have no excuses. We're not talking about unbelievers who have never known the truth about God, or those living in faraway lands where the gospel has never been preached.

The next verse continues along these lines:

Rom 1:21

21 For although *they knew God,* they neither glorified him as God *nor gave thanks to him,* but their thinking *became* futile, and their foolish hearts were darkened.

It says "*although they knew God...*" this implies they knew God, personally. It does not say "when they knew *about* God". There is a world of difference between knowing someone and knowing *about* someone. In high school, I had to write a term paper about someone. I wrote about George Romney, the former governor of Michigan. Through much research, I knew quite a bit *about* George Romney. I did not know him, though. I never met him. The Scripture says they *knew God!* This means there was a definite time when they did know God personally. The unbeliever does not have this knowledge. They can only know about God, or that there is a God, but they don't personally know Him, yet. These folks knew God but did not glorify Him as God. Does that happen in the Bible? Yes. Remember, there were ten lepers who all got healed, but only one returned to thank Jesus. Jesus said to that one, "your faith has made you whole". The other nine never said thank you.

Rom 1:22-23

22 Although they claimed to be wise, they became fools

23 and *exchanged* the glory of the immortal God for images made to look like mortal man and birds and animals and reptiles. (NIV)

The word *exchanged* means: *to make different, change, exchange.* We already know that in ancient Rome there were 420 different temples, each to a different god or goddess. These entities had different likenesses, some images were of a winged horse, and some were of centaurs. Some images were of a woman with snakes for her hair. There were all kinds of images: half man, half ox; half woman, half fish as were mermaids, and so forth. There were many kinds of images that they bowed down to worship. People have done this for centuries. Even during the exodus, the people of God asked Aaron to make an image for them to worship. They subsequently bowed down to the golden calf Aaron made. This happened while Moses was in the very presence of God. The people took their melted gold earrings, made an image, and they then declared this was the God who delivered them from Pharaoh. Their foolish heart was darkened. They knew God but did not glorify God as God, and neither were they thankful to Yahweh. They thanked their jewelry! They exchanged the glory of God for the glory of an image made like unto a corruptible animal, a four-footed beast.

In other cultures, they still carve out images and bow down to them. They attribute their statue with their fortune, good or bad. It was their god who made the disaster pass by. It was an angry god who wiped out the city with the volcano. It needs appeasing to keep from erupting again. The sun god, the rain god, and the wind god, all get worshipped in various cultures. They should know better. The heavens declare God's handiwork.

They exchanged the truth about God for a lie. They knew God as Creator but did not credit Him as thus. Is this a *homosexual* problem? No, it is universally a human problem. No culture or ethnic entity has a corner on the market of ignoring and replacing God.

Rom 1:23-24

23 and exchanged the glory of the immortal God for images made to look like mortal man and birds and animals and reptiles.

24 *Therefore God gave them over* in the sinful desires of their hearts to sexual impurity for the degrading of their bodies with one another.

Rom 1: 24 says "Therefore *God gave them over*, He *gave them up*". This is a powerful statement. Considering how patient and merciful God is with humanity, it would take an incredible amount of provocation for God to throw His hands up in the air about someone, declaring He has given up dealing with their life and heart. Yet here, God got fed up. Considering God's nature, it would take quite a bit before God simply removes His hands. People sin and sin and sin, and God keeps reaching out and reaching out and reaching out. How many times has God forgiven us?

Romans 2:4 declares that it is the goodness, the kindness of God that leads us to repentance. It is because God is so good and allows the prodigal child time to see the foolishness of a life without God, that, if we will ever do so, we finally turn home to God. One deacon in our church said, "Everyone goes to Heaven!" We looked at him like he was nuts, then he said smiling, "But not everyone gets to stay." It is not God, the One Who so loves the world that gave us up. We firmly, openly, and rebelliously rejected God. God doesn't keep us out of Heaven, we do. It was God who made the Way possible.

The people addressed had become so steeped in idol worship; that there was no turning back to God. Therefore, God gave them up. It is a declaration: "OK, if that's what you want, have it!" These are the people to whom God is speaking. The scripture does not just begin Romans with verse 26. There is the groundwork of context laid first. These people do not just one day wake up and say "Gee, let's have sex with members of our own sex today for a change of pace." First, they *exchange* their worship from true to false. They start off by *exchanging* their God. They *become* vain in their imaginations. They *exchange* the Glory of God for images, which are shadows and types of real things, but not truth. They *exchange* the truth for a lie. They had the truth. They rejected the truth. These folks were heterosexuals. The next thing they *exchange* is their object of lust. But not until after God gave up on them.

God gave up on them when they were heterosexuals!

We are not addressing homosexuals. We are addressing idolaters; those who made a deliberate decision, while fully knowing who God is and were without an excuse. They decided nonetheless to worship something other than God.

God gave them over *to the sinful desires of their hearts*. So now whatever their hearts decide to do, that is what they will do. Their hearts are not listening to God because God gave them up and is not speaking to their hearts. What they will listen to is the sinful desires, or as the King James Version says, *"the lust in their own hearts"*. That is *lust*, not love.

Now comes verse 25.

Rom 1:25

25 They *exchanged* the *truth* of God for a *lie* and worshiped and served created things rather than the Creator-- who is forever praised.

Watch this verse carefully! They exchange the truth of God for a lie. They are not listening to God the Father; He's given up on them. God has removed His hand from them. So now they are not having anything to do with truth. Now they listen exclusively to the Father of Lies. This is becoming a very depraved people. They worship and *serve* the creature *more than* the Creator. This does not say they do not serve the Creator at all. It says they worship their idol and serve their idol/ creature more than God.

Now comes verse 26.

Rom 1:26

26 *Because of this*, God gave them over to shameful lusts. Even their women exchanged natural relations for unnatural ones.

Because of *what*? Because God hates homosexuals? No! *God gave them up because they gave up God!*

Rom 1:27

27 *In the same way*, the men also abandoned natural relations with women and were *inflamed with lust* for one another. Men committed indecent acts with other men and received in themselves the due penalty for their perversion.

In the same way, also the men, these heterosexual men *leave* their wives and girlfriends, leaving what is natural for a heterosexual man in order to burn in all-encompassing, inflaming, overwhelming passionate *lust* committing indecent acts with one another. Who are they walking with? It is not God.

We have not finished looking at these idolaters with their sex orgies. There are more verses to come! They did not merely get to a place where they had sex with each other and quit.

Now comes verse 28.

Rom 1:28

28 Furthermore, *since they did not think it worthwhile to retain the knowledge of God,* he gave them over to a depraved mind; to do what ought not to be done.

God's manner of giving up on them was to take His hand off them. Therefore, they were free to follow the way the flesh leads when it is not submitted to God. They did not merely have sex out of lust for each other. What else did they do? How else did they behave? What other attitudes did they have? The New American Standard Version puts it this way:

Rom 1:28-32

28 And just as they did not see fit to acknowledge God any longer, God gave them over to a depraved mind, to do those things which are not proper,

29 being *filled* with *all unrighteousness,* wickedness, greed, evil; *full of* envy, murder, strife, deceit, malice; they are gossips,

30 slanderers, *haters of God,* insolent, arrogant, boastful, inventors of evil, disobedient to parents,

31 without understanding, untrustworthy, unloving, unmerciful.

32 and, although they know the ordinance of God, that those who practice such things are worthy of death, they not only do the same but also give hearty approval to those who practice them. [NAS]

These folks are now *filled* with ALL unrighteousness. There is no room for God in such a life. After the sentence says these folks are filled with *all* unrighteousness, it goes on to describe *all* they are *filled* with. They are *filled* with *all* wickedness, greed, and evil. They are *filled* with *all* envy, murder, strife, deceit, and malice. They are full of envy and murder and strife. They are not nice to be around! They are *filled* with *all* gossip, slander, insolence, arrogance, and boasting. It is no surprise that they are *haters of God*, inventors of evil, disobedient to parents, without understanding, untrustworthy, unloving, and unmerciful. Additionally, the King James Version reveals they are filled with *all* backbiting.

The verb tense in these scriptures is in the past tense, so Paul refers to a group of people who forsook God in a time past. Now though there are many ancient groups that worshiped idols, scripture itself reveals this event, *particularly* among the *ancient Hebrews*. No other group knew God the way they did, particularly in the Exodus, when God's presence went with them as a pillar of cloud by day and a pillar of fire by night.

They had the Glory, in the manifest presence of God right there in their camp, yet they still exchanged what they had (the Glory of God) for an image of a beast. While Moses was on Mount Sinai receiving the law on two carved stone tablets, the people rose up to play. The play referred to was to throw an out-of-control orgy and sacrifice with an idol of gold they made from their earrings.

Psalms 106:13-14

They soon forgot his works; they waited not for his counsel:

14 But lusted exceedingly in the wilderness, and tempted God in the desert. (KJV)

Psalms 81:11-13

But *my people would not hearken to my voice, and Israel would none of me.*

12 *So I gave them up unto their own hearts' lust:* [and] they walked in their own counsels. 13 Oh that my people had hearkened unto me, [and] Israel had walked in my ways! (KJV)

Psalms 106:15-23

And he (God) gave them their request but sent leanness into their soul.

16 They envied Moses also in the camp, [and] Aaron the saint of the LORD...

19 They *made a calf in Horeb* and *worshiped the molten image.*

20 Thus *they changed their glory into the similitude of an ox that eateth grass.*

21 They forgot God their savior, which had done great things in Egypt...

23 Therefore he said that he would destroy them, had not Moses his chosen stood before him in the breach, to turn away his wrath, lest he should destroy [them]. (KJV)

1 Corinthians 10:1-11

Moreover, brethren, I would not that ye should be ignorant, how that all our fathers were under the cloud, and all passed through the sea;

2 And were all baptized unto Moses in the cloud and in the sea.

3 And did all eat the same spiritual meat.

4 And did all drink the same spiritual drink: for they drank of that spiritual Rock that followed them: and that Rock was Christ.

5 But with many of them God was not well pleased: for they were overthrown in the wilderness.

6 Now these things were our examples, to the intent *we should not lust after evil things, as they also lusted.*

7 *Neither be ye idolaters, as [were] some of them; as it is written, the people sat down to eat and drink, and rose up to play.*

8 Neither *let us commit fornication, as some of them committed, and fell in one day three and twenty thousand.*

9 Neither let us tempt Christ, as some of them also tempted, and were destroyed of serpents.

10 Neither murmur ye, as some of them also murmured, and were destroyed of the destroyer.

11 Now all these things happened unto them for ensamples: and they are written for our admonition, upon whom the ends of the world are come. (KJV)

The same apostle Paul who wrote the letter to the Romans wrote this letter to the Corinthians to tell them that ancient Israel was guilty of idolatry, out-of-control burning lust, and illicit sex.

Acts 7:35 - 44

Stephen before he was martyred declared that *ancient Israel refused to listen to God* or Moses, even though God showed them signs and miracles. They still became idolatrous, not only with the golden calf, but with the false gods of other nations, serving Moloch, and the god Remphan, figures *which they made to worship.* This is another retelling of how ancient Israel forsook the glory of God and exchanged it for images and idols.

They refused the instructions of the law given them by God through Moses by saying, "Who made thee a ruler and a judge?" The hearts of ancient Israel kept lusting after the forbidden things from which they were once delivered.

Acts 7:37-43

This is that Moses, which said unto the children of Israel, A prophet shall the Lord your God raise up unto you of your brethren, like unto me; him shall ye hear.

38 This is he, that was in the church in the wilderness with the angel which spoke to him in the mount Sinai, and with our fathers: who received the lively oracles to give unto us:

39 To whom *our fathers would not obey*, but thrust him from them, and in their *hearts turned back again into Egypt*,

40 Saying unto Aaron, *make us gods to go before us*: for as for this Moses, which brought us out of the land of Egypt, we know not what is become of him. 41 And *they made a calf in those days*, and *offered sacrifice unto the idol*, and *rejoiced in the works of their own hands*.

42 Then *God turned, and gave them up* to worship the host of heaven; as it is written in the book of the prophets, O ye house of Israel, have ye offered to me slain beasts and sacrifices by the space of forty years in the wilderness?

43 Yea, ye took up the *tabernacle of Moloch*, and the star of *your god Remphan*, figures which *ye made to worship them...* (KJV)

Many other Scriptures testify to this same thing:

- Jeremiah 2:5, 11; 18:15; 19:4-5, Deuteronomy 32:13-32, Exodus 32:1-35,

1 Kings 12:31, and Hosea 4:14 for example point out that ancient Israel in the time of the Exodus and in other periods of their history worshiped the idols of the nations around them. Those *fertility cults demanded sexual sacrifices* with male and female cultic priests. Clearly above all other peoples, these are the people who knew God and did not honor Him as God and neither were they thankful, at least not in their ancient history.

So clearly Romans 1 is not addressing gay people at all, but idolatrous, rebellious ancient Israel at the lowest points of its history. They gave up the glory and presence of the Living God, to run after the false idols they made. And as they worshiped those pagan idols with out-of-control sexual orgies and sacrifices, God gave up on them. In the case of the Exodus, it was only the prayerful intercession of Moses (whom they rejected) that stopped the Hebrew God from wiping Israel off the map and raising up a newly separated people from Moses alone.

"THIS IS NOT THE STORY OF THE GAY CHRISTIAN"

These people listed in Romans 1 are *filled* with *all* wickedness. This is not the testimony of gay Christians. You can't be a Christian, a follower of Christ, and be filled with *all* wickedness at the same time. The person listed in Romans 1 is *filled* with *all* covetousness. This is not the character of a Christian believer, gay or otherwise.

They are filled with all maliciousness, filled with all murder. We're not talking about a gay Christian couple who is walking with and worshiping Jesus. You can't pull verses 26-27 out of context and still get a true picture of what situation is addressed. Some have tried to use these verses to say God hates homosexuals. That is not a true picture of what is shown in the whole chapter. God is not condemning gays, and one's sexual orientation is not even at issue. At odds with God here is the idolater who has pushed God out of their life, even though they know better. They began to go downward in their thinking because they reject God. They do not even want to retain God in their knowledge. Therefore, they are filled with *all* wickedness.

As the people listed go down this slippery slope, Romans says they are *haters* of God! Rev. Frank Scott shared with me that this was the passage that rather condemns him as a gay man, set him free. He knew if nothing else he was not a hater of God. God was his best friend, and he loved the Lord. It was obvious in his life the Lord loved him, too. No one could now count how many people Pastor Frank has helped and led to Christ. He is *not* a hater of God. He is Christian. He is gay. He is called, equipped, and anointed.

Though so many people try to say this Romans passage proves that God hates homosexuals, yet this was the passage that proved God did not hate homosexuals. It became clear to Rev. Scott that he was not being addressed here at all. This was the passage that brought him true freedom in Christ.

This passage is used by Christians to deny gay people the right to membership.

It is used to prevent gay people from having their relationship of love blessed, Communion is withheld, employment is withheld; all because people think this passage says something it does not. Paul was speaking to first-century Christians with knowledge of ancient Israel's history. They were aware that at the time of the Exodus, the people who knew God exchanged the glory of God for an image made from their earrings. They also entered revelry and out-of-control carnality as they worshiped an idol of a golden ox. Moses was shocked when he came off the mountain with God's laws written on the two stone tablets by the finger of God. These people were out of control. It is this encounter that Paul addresses when he says they exchanged several things for another. They exchanged the glory of God for demonic idol worship; they exchanged sexual appropriateness with their spouse with burning out-of-control lust for one another. Men and men, women and women, primarily heterosexuals, whose burning, out-of-control lust brought them shame and judgment as they exchanged what was naturally inherent to them for an illicit affair.

It doesn't matter if a person is gay or has any other orientation. What matters is if they belong to Jesus. If they belong to Jesus, the fruit of the Spirit will be evident and growing.

The *fruit of the Spirit is not heterosexuality*. The fruit of the Spirit is love, joy, peace, longsuffering, gentleness, goodness, faith, meekness, temperance. (Gal 5:22-23)

One who is Christ's sheep knows His voice. They worship and serve the Creator rather than our old selfish nature. God is looking for those who would seek His face. God is looking for worshippers who will worship Him in Spirit and in truth. Our lives should reflect His glory. If it doesn't, ask the Lord where we miss the mark, and walk in the light of His insight. Walking with God has benefits. Peace, joy, love, insight for living and destiny fulfilled are only a few.

God declares the fields are ripe for harvest. Our mandate is to tell the good news of God's unconditional love for all. Who can God send? God is looking for disciple-makers. Only those with God's heartbeat of love can be effective. It is now time to extend a hand of love and friendship to others, inviting them to come on this journey with us and our loving God. That's how we make disciples of Jesus.

All this Scriptural insight came about as the Holy Spirit moved among the gay community, even in the early years.

1 CORINTHIANS / 1 TIMOTHY *Greek Happens*

Depending on the Bible translation one is reading, there are two passages in the New Testament that are frequently cited against homosexuality. Interestingly enough both these passages use the same two Greek words that are sometimes translated as the word *homosexual*. These passages are found in 1 Corinthians 6:9 and 1 Timothy 1:10. In the King James Version they read as follows:

1 Cor 6:9-10

> 9 Know ye not that the unrighteous shall not inherit the kingdom of God? Be not deceived: neither fornicators, nor idolaters, nor adulterers, nor effeminate, nor abusers of themselves with mankind,

> 10 Nor thieves, nor covetous, nor drunkards, nor revilers, nor extortioners, shall inherit the kingdom of God. (KJV)

1 Tim 1:9-10

> 9 Knowing this, that the law is not made for a righteous man, but for the lawless and disobedient, for the ungodly and for sinners, for unholy and profane, for murderers of fathers and murderers of mothers, for man slayers,

> 10 For whore mongers, for them that defile themselves with mankind, for men stealers, for liars, for perjured persons, and if there be any other thing that is contrary to sound doctrine; (KJV)

In these passages, there are two words used that come into question. Some translations combine the words into one word as if they were one concept. Other translations give a plethora of options in their choice of translating these two words into English. Since this is the New Testament, the words are originally written in Greek, and the corresponding numbers for them in the *Strong's Concordance* are:

3120 **malakos** (mal-ak-os'); of *uncertain affinity; soft*, i.e., fine (clothing).

and # 733 *arsenokoites* (ar-sen-ok-oy'-tace); from 730 and 2845

When researching these Greek New Testament words, it becomes apparent they are rarely used at all in the Bible.

The word *malakos* [# 3120] literally means *soft*.

The other word, *arsenokoites* [# 733] is a word Paul made up. The first time this word is used in ancient Greek literature is in I Corinthians. Paul's word *arsenokoites*, is a compound word like Obamacare, or lady killer as pointed out by Daniel Helminiak [9].

For instance, is a lady killer a man who sweeps women off their feet? Is it a person with a gun who targets women? Or is it a homicidal female? Context is everything.

This compound word in the Bible which was made up by Paul is one he expects his readers to understand. But other than these two cited texts, this word is not used anywhere else in the Bible. The two words Paul compounded together were the words [# 730] which means *lifting*, and the word [# 2845] which means *couch*. Therefore, the literal meaning of these two words is: *lift couch: arsenokoites*. The word *arsenokoites* is not seen in the literature for another four hundred years.

Today if we said God is "awful," people would think we were angry with God and you better watch what you say. Yet four hundred years ago the word awful meant awe-inspiring, full of awe. In four hundred years the word has had a complete reversal of meaning, from something good to something bad.

Paul assumed his hearers would understand the word he was coining. But today, there is great debate about the meaning of lift *couch* (*arsenokoites*). English Bibles today translate this word in a myriad of ways. We will look at some of these conflicting translations.

We will break down I Corinthians 6: 9, using the *Strong's* numbers, to note the location of these words.

1 Corinthians 6:9

> 9 Know ye not that the unrighteous shall not inherit the kingdom of God? Be not deceived: neither fornicators, nor idolaters, nor *adulterers*, nor *effeminate* [3120 *malakos*] [10], nor *abusers of themselves with mankind* [733 *arsenokoites*] ...

Notice that the words in question, [#3120] *malakos* and [#733] *arsenokoites*, are together in sequence and follow the word *adulterers*. That is important to notice because in some translations you will never recognize the words unless you know they are whatever follows *adulterers*. Many times, the translation will combine both words into one word as if they convey the same concept. In such a case I list it under the first word since only one is given. Also, if the translators change their definition/ translation of a word between I Corinthians 6:9 and the same word [#733] *arsenokoites* in I Timothy 1:10, the difference is noted.

Many conservative church leaders, pastors, and Christian writers conclude that the words *soft* and *lift couch* (which literally follow the word *adulterers*) condemn all homosexuals under all conditions and that under no circumstances can a gay person ever get into Heaven. They state that as long as a person is a homosexual, they can never be Christian. They make that assumption by stating that neither the *effeminate* nor the *abusers of themselves with mankind*, etc., shall inherit the kingdom of God.

Therefore, as we list and study the various English translations, we will see that the translators rarely agree on what these two words mean among themselves. Often, they ignore the one word, *malakos* as if it was not there. And even within the same translation, the word *arsenokoites* is not translated as the same thing consistently. It seems to mean one thing in I Corinthians, and another in I Timothy. One thing is clear, though. In ancient Greek, there was no noun to express homosexuality. If the ancient world wanted to talk about homosexuality, they would have used verbs, to express specific sexual activity. There was no noun "homosexual" because the concept of a person whose orientation is gay was unknown in that day. Therefore, anytime one of these words is translated as homosexual, it is a mistranslation since the word "homosexual" did not even exist until the nineteenth century. Let's look at several of the translations we have in English. They are conveniently placed in a table to identify how the two Greek words are translated.

Remember in each case we're looking at the two words that follow *adulterers* in I Corinthians 6:9.

ENGLISH TRANSLATION 3120 MALAKOS 733 ARSENOKOITES:

KING JAMES VERSION

EFFEMINATE

ABUSERS OF THEMSELVES

WITH MANKIND/

I TIM. 1:10 *THEM THAT DEFILE THEMSELVES WITH MANKIND*

NIV

MALE PROSTITUTES

HOMOSEXUAL OFFENDERS /

I TIM 1:10: *PERVERTS*

LIVING BIBLE

HOMOSEXUALS

INTERLINEAR BIBLE

ABUSERS

HOMOSEXUALS

REVISED

SEXUAL PERVERTS

I TIM.1:10 *SODOMITES*

J.B. PHILLIPS

EFFEMINATE

PERVERT

I TIM. 1:10 *SEXUALLY UNCONTROLLED OR PERVERTS*

AMPLIFIED

THOSE WHO PARTICIPATE IN HOMOSEXUALITY

I TIMOTHY1:10: *THOSE WHO ABUSE THEMSELVES WITH MEN*

NEW ENGLISH BIBLE

HOMOSEXUAL PERVERSION

I TIM.1:10 *PERVERTS*

NEW KING JAMES

HOMOSEXUALS

[EXPLAINED AS *CATAMITES* IN FOOTNOTES]

SODOMITES [EXPLAINED AS *MALE HOMOSEXUALS* IN FOOTNOTES]

NEW AMERICAN STANDARD BIBLE

EFFEMINATE

HOMOSEXUALS

BARCLAY

SENSUALISTS

HOMOSEXUALS

GOOD NEWS

HOMOSEXUAL PERVERTS

I TIM. 1:10: *SEXUAL PERVERTS*

ST. JOSEPH NEW CATHOLIC EDITION

EFFEMINATE

SODOMITES

The King James Version translates the word # 3120 *malakos, soft,* word as *effeminate.* The NIV translates this same word as a *male prostitute.* Those are totally different concepts. For the word # 733, *arsenokoites, lift couch,* the King James Version calls them *abusers of themselves with mankind.* The NIV calls them *homosexual offenders.* These are different concepts. If I said a person was an abuser of themselves with mankind, that might imply that they somehow abuse their bodies with men. That could be a male or a female person. Abuse is the issue. If I say the same person is a homosexual offender, I could mean they are a gay person who got a traffic violation. A homosexual offender is a person who breaks the law, and also happens to be gay. It could be a gay person who ran a red light and got pulled over by the police. That may not be what NIV had in mind but nonetheless the definition still applies.

After *the Living Bible* says *adulterers,* it then says *homosexuals.* It only gives one word, so it combines *malakos* and *arsenokoites* into one word, the word *homosexuals.* As far as they are concerned, both words, both individuals being spoken about, are homosexuals.

The Interlinear Bible translates *malakos,* the word *soft* as *abusers.* It is interesting that they are saying the word *soft* is an *abuser.* You would not think that the person called *soft* would be the person who would be an abuser but rather the abused. Usually, an abuser is someone who is hardened and rough and abuses others verbally or physically. Someone who has been abused would not think their abuser was soft, milquetoast, or a pushover. Then they take the word *arsenokoites* and translate it, *homosexuals*. Those are two different groups of people: *abusers* and *homosexuals*.

They do not even specify what these abusers abuse. Are they wife-beaters? Are they drug abusers? Do they belong to over-eaters anonymous because they are abusers of food? All this from the word *soft*.

Then we have the Revised Version. They put the two words together after adulterers and call them *sexual perverts*. Sexual perverts bring up a completely different concept. If I said to you that person is a sexual pervert, what would you think I meant? A sexual pervert is often referring to someone who perhaps molests little girls. That would usually be a heterosexual male since statistically they by far have the greatest numbers of child molestation cases in the courts. Homosexuality is not a perversion per se, since it occurs naturally among not only humans but in the animal kingdom as well. Dogs, mice, ducks, penguins, swans, and countless other species have seen homosexual pairing occur among them. So, though it is not the majority, it is a variation among the norms. Child abuse is not a norm, whether it is sexual or otherwise. Serial rapists would also be among the sexual perverts. These again would in the majority of cases be heterosexual men.

The J.B. Phillips translation translates *malakos, soft,* as *effeminate,* and the word *arsenokoites, lift couch* as a *pervert.* The word pervert brings up a totally different concept again. If I were to ask a police officer to show me the records of all the perverts they have on file, they probably would have lots of individuals to bring up, but they would not necessarily be homosexuals. What is a pervert? What would be the definition among different groups of people in different cultures throughout the centuries?

Some people might consider the cultures of their neighboring nations as perverted. For instance, ancient Israel's neighbors worshiped Molech, and sacrificed their children as living burnt offerings in the fire. In the days when the ancient nation Israel was walking in obedience to God, like under King David or Hezekiah, the practice of worshiping Molech and burning your children certainly seemed perverted, as it does now.

The word *soft, malakos,* being translated *effeminate,* makes you wonder what are the translators trying to convey? Do they mean that if a man is just a little effeminate that he can never get into Heaven under any conditions? There are many happily married heterosexual men who are a little bit effeminate. They might be the househusband and a nurturing caretaker of their children. They might just walk in an "unmanly" way, whatever that is. Maybe they don't like football, sports, or fixing cars, but do like to take care of the house and are generally more sensitive, nurturing, and considerate. What is implied in translating this word as *effeminate? Does it* mean that every effeminate man, no matter to what degree, is going to hell? That's what some would imply. As Christians mature, they become gentler and meeker. Paul said when he was weak, then he was strong. Does that make Paul effeminate? If so, he never could get to Heaven according to this mistranslation.

The word *effeminate* does not imply any sexual conduct or behavior whatsoever! Neither does it mean a homosexual! Furthermore, the Bible is not implying that an effeminate person is going to hell! Even modern Bible translations cannot agree on what these ancient words meant. Christians walk on thin ice by condemning homosexuals based on these two scriptural passages.

The Amplified Bible lumps the two words together and says, *"those who participate in homosexuality".* There is a world of difference between people who participate in homosexuality, meaning have same-sex sexual activity, and those who are homosexual. Someone can be a homosexual and never have a sexual experience. Likewise, a predominately heterosexually oriented person could end up in a homosexual or homo-genital sexual encounter. It is a common event among heterosexual men in prison. Being a homosexual is not about sexual activity. It is about whom one is attracted to, likely to fall in love with, and with whom they want to spend their life. A person's sexual orientation defines which gender they gravitate towards. For some that is exclusively someone of the opposite sex. For others that is never the case. When the Amplified says *those who participate in homosexuality,* it does not have to refer to a gay person at all.

The New English Bible lumps *malakos* and *arsenokoites* together and says those who are guilty of *homosexual perversion* will not inherit God's kingdom. My question is, what is a *homosexual* perversion? It would imply that a homosexual who is not a pervert is okay. But one who is a pervert is condemned in this passage. Who is that person? Would it be perverted for a homosexual to act like a heterosexual, since that perverts their innate nature?

The New King James Version does something different. They translate the first word following adulterers, *malakos, soft,* as the word *homosexuals,* and the second word, *arsenokoites, lift couch* as a *sodomite.* In the footnotes of the New King James Version, Spirit-Filled Life Bible [11] the footnote for the word translated homosexual helps explain how *malakos, soft* became homosexual by defining it as *catamite; those submitting to homosexuals.* I wonder if that footnote was clarification or confusion because *malakos* now goes from *homosexual* to *catamite.* This definition in their footnote now changes the word *homosexual* to a catamite, or as they say, *one who submits to a homosexual.* Again, there is a big difference between a homosexual and someone who submits to one. Children when molested by a relative may do so out of fear and intimidation by the adult but that does not mean they were willing participants. People can submit without giving consent. The latter person identified as a catamite is not identified any longer by sexual orientation. There is no longer a clue as to whether they are heterosexual, gay, or something else.

Then the word *sodomite* is explained in their footnote as *male homosexuals.* The biblical book of Ezekiel explained Sodomites as people who were inhospitable [12] and arrogant. In fact, the people of God are referred to as the rulers of Sodom in

Isaiah 1:10. Then the instruction God gives for them to redeem themselves is found in verses 15-20. In the midst of that passage, in Isaiah 1:17, they are told to relieve the oppressed.

The New American Standard Bible translates the first word in I Cor. 6:9 following *adulterers,* the word *malakos, soft,* as *effeminate;* and they translate the second word, *arsenokoites, lift couch,* as *homosexuals.* This of course is *homosexuals,* unqualified. Any homosexual is referred to, whether they have ever participated in homogenital activity of any kind or not. It does not differentiate between a monogamous loving relationship, and stable loving home life, a series of one-night stands, serial weekend affairs, or half-hour incognito escapades in the dark. Yet a true homosexual is not a verb, a description of sexual activity, but a noun — a person. It is a person who lives their life out as does any other human being but realizes they are attracted to someone of the same sex, rather than, or more than the opposite sex. A bisexual is a person who is attracted to both men and women. This noun does not mean any of these attractions are acted upon.

In ancient Greek, the concept of homosexuality was unknown as a noun but was expressed as a verb. It is expressed as a behavior, as certain specific sexual activities, rather than as a specific kind of person. To state that *lift couch* is a homosexually oriented person, with no more description than that, is a gross injustice.

The word heterosexual as a noun does not tell me whether this person is single and celibate or a prostitute. It does not explain whether this heterosexual is a 90-year-old widower or a 10-year-old child. All can be heterosexuals. It does not state whether they are good to their spouse, or not. It does not tell me whether they commit adultery or have been faithful to a spouse over the years. Very little information is conveyed by the word heterosexual. It only tells me they are attracted to people of the opposite sex, nothing more. Likewise, the noun homosexual tells me no more information than that. Therefore, it is a faulty assumption to state that all homosexuals are excluded from the Kingdom of God, regardless of any other factors, such as whether they have made Jesus Christ the Lord of their life or not. Not only is it possible to be Christian and gay, but it is also a reality for untold numbers already worshiping in congregations around the world. It would take very little effort to meet thousands of gay Christians who love God.

In the Barclay translation *malakos* is translated *sensualists* and *arsenokoites* is translated as *homosexuals*.

The Good News Bible combines both words in I Cor. 6:9 to call them *homosexual perverts*, then changes their mind about the word *arsenokoites* in I Timothy 1:10 and calls them *sexual perverts*.

Homosexual perverts are not the same as *sexual perverts* [Good News]. *Those who participate in homosexuality* are not the same *as those who abuse themselves with men*, which could be female prostitutes, or a variety of other life situations; [Amplified]. Bible translators are not consistent even within their own translations, much less as various different translations are checked. It leads to a great deal of confusion. No wonder when these two obscure words are used so rarely, and then as in the case of *arsenokoites*, the word Paul coined to describe a particular situation in Corinth.

When some Christians try to say, "Well the Bible says homosexuals are not getting into heaven!" the question then remains to which Bible translation are you referring?

Sometimes translators look at a word and try to figure out what it means by looking at its usage in other secular writings of the time. But that option is not available for *arsenokoites* since it is only used twice.

The word *malakos* is used in a few other places in the Bible. In each other case, the word # 3120 in *Strong's* New Testament is translated *soft* in both the King James Version and the New American Standard Version.

Matt 11:8

8 "But what did you go out to see? A man dressed in *soft* clothing. Behold, those who wear *soft* clothing are in kings' palaces. (NAS)

The word means soft. It is not translated that they are wearing sexually perverted clothing. It is not translated as they are wearing male prostitute clothing in a king's houses. It is not abusive clothing. This clothing in a king's house does not participate in homosexuality. It is not catamite clothing. It is not effeminate clothing. So why is it translated as all these other things in I Corinthians, or ignored altogether as it is coupled with the word arsenokoites, as if malakos doesn't matter?

WHO ARE THE PEOPLE SO DESCRIBED?

When Paul wrote to the church at Corinth in the first century, it would have been obvious to them what he was talking about. His coined new word had meaning to those in that day. Paul then went on to say this included some of those within that first-century church. They would have been able to look around the congregation and nod their heads in agreement; yes, some of us were like that. They would know from personal experience and be able to say yes, I was that. They would know whether they had been a *lift couch* or not.

So now we go back into archeology and anthropology and look at first-century Greek and Roman culture and see what Paul could have been addressing. A modern understanding of a so-called "homosexual lifestyle" was not what Paul was talking about.

He was not addressing gay couples living together, setting up a home, checking accounts, and living with one another. But he was addressing something they all knew about. Many Corinthians could indeed say they had been very familiar with the life Paul was talking about. Paul said such were some of you, and they agreed.

The social norms of the first century Greek and Roman cultures are well documented in the writings from that era, as well as by many noted historians such as John Boswell [13] and Robin Scroggs.[14] It has long been established historically that in that era adolescent boys were considered sexually desirable by older men. The culture glorified the youthful male body. Once they grew a beard the attraction was over, and the desirability was gone as an object of romanticized sex. Men routinely engaged 'boys', i.e., adolescent males. Youth was a more established requirement for the male than for the female among prostitutes; for women could be considered desirable in middle age whereas before the age of twenty a boy already ceased to be desirable. Greek men seem to have regarded the presence of hair upon the cheeks, thighs, and hindquarters of maturing youth with intense sexual distaste. Once the boy became a teenager, started to sprout facial hair, no longer looked boyish, and started to develop as a man, his sexual desirability to other men was over. This was a norm within that culture.

Of course, there were still gay men whose attraction was to the adult male, such as the emperor Galba, 68 AD, or the Roman Emperor Hadrian (ruled 117-138 ad) for example. Royston Lambert describes the relationship Emperor Hadrian had with his youthful lover Antinous in his well-researched book: *Beloved and God: The Story of Hadrian and Antinous.*[15]

However, within the culture, of Greek and Roman citizens, in this man-boy relationship, the boy was also expected to get married, raise his own children, and work in a trade. He was not expected to continue on in homogenital liaisons with other men. This man-boy attraction was widespread and commonplace. Neither the boy nor the man was considered to be homosexual in orientation. It was more of power exploitation on the part of the man, since often boys were seduced then dropped later, or were exploited slaves, abused without rights.

Although the activity was homosexual in its genital arrangement, neither partner was considered to be a gay person in the modern sense of that word. The man in fact would probably be heterosexually married, expected his marriage to remain intact, and expected the seduction of the boy to be a transient affair. Scroggs notes [16] the youth bestow a sexual favor by giving his body to the man but expected to receive favors or gifts of various sorts. Small animals such as hares or birds seem to be common. It was the adult who selected the partner, who determined what happened in the sexual encounter, and who received the sexual gratification. Adult males seem to have often moved from youth to youth. Whenever, in their judgment, the youth was no longer desirable, they were dropped without choice in the matter. The personhood of the boy is secondary to his personal attractiveness. This would naturally lead to personal humiliation when one boy was rejected for another. The boy would be left feeling abused and dehumanized by such a temporary sexual relationship. Its impermanence, inequality, and humiliation after being rejected, could leave emotional scars on even the most resilient of youngsters. Scroggs [17] quotes Plutarch stating, "Young men not naturally vicious, who have been lured or forced into yielding and letting themselves be abused, forever after mistrust and hate no one on earth more than the men who so served them and, if an opportunity offers, they take a terrible revenge."[18]

In addition to voluntary sexual encounters between the free-born men and boys were various forms of slave prostitution. There were brothels taxed by the city in Athens, for instance. Some slave boys were sold into these brothels. Other household slaves were also used sexually by their masters. Scroggs notes how it was common to castrate these youths to keep their youthful appearance, increasing their usefulness for sexual activity.[19]

A famous example was Nero's treatment of his slave boy Sporus. He had Sporus castrated, dressed in women's clothes, given a woman's name, and publicly married the slave as a wife. The society of Rome did not think the relationship was all that uncommon or unusual. But since Nero was so widely hated, his opponents often lamented it was too bad Nero's father had not married a lad as Nero had done, instead of Nero's mother.

Beyond the situations cited with youth who were seduced for their charms or slaves who were forced into brothels or sexually compromising situations, there were still other well-known situations in ancient Greece and Rome. One was the free-born male hustler. This situation was socially looked upon with disfavor. It seems that once a boy got used to gifts and money for selling his body, it became an easy way to continue in a lucrative financial exchange. Scroggs sites a case made against Timarchus [20] in which the young man is portrayed to the jury as an insatiable lustful degenerate who prostitutes himself over and over to older men. The prosecutor, Aeschines, admits he himself is a lover of beautiful young boys but makes a distinction between what is socially acceptable and how Timarchus has crossed the line. The prosecutor states "to be in love with those who are beautiful and chaste is the experience of a kindhearted and generous soul; but to hire for money and indulge in licentiousness is the act of a man who is wanton and ill-bred." It was okay for an adult male to seduce a previously chaste, beautiful boy, but if the boy really wanted the money and the sex, he was ill-bred and wanton. This was the complaint against Timarchus. The point being Timarchus was not under compulsion to have such sex for money but sought it out deliberately. Aeschines' prosecution speech would only make sense if he thought the jury would understand the logic he presented.

Additionally, Cicero accused Mark Anthony of being a wanton hustler. Apparently, according to Cicero's version, this great lover of Cleopatra was a male prostitute in his earlier days. Both Cicero and the Jewish historian Josephus report this is to be true.[21]

In all these cases we are not talking about homosexual orientation, but about heterosexuals acting upon homogenital erotic behavior.

Once a person became a Christian, however, they come under a new law. No longer are we under the survival of the fittest, but we are commanded to love our neighbor as ourselves. Once the adult man became a Christian and with the Holy Spirit guiding him, it became very difficult to justify sexually abusing and seducing children and maintaining an exploitative power relationship over them. It doesn't take too long to understand, considering the magnitude of this socially approved exploitative relationship, that this is likely what Paul is addressing.

They could nod in agreement when Paul said, such were some of you, but now you've changed, now you're different. Now perhaps the older man is taking the boy under his wing as a son, and genuinely caring for him, instead of exploiting his young apprentice or slave.

Therefore, it is possible, not totally conclusive, that *arsenokoites* could have been this adult heterosexual male who had temporary sexual encounters with a male adolescent. And *malakos, soft,* could be the youth who was being used sexually. He could be soft because he was not yet developed as a man.

So *malakos* and *arsenokoites* could have been referring to the relationship between this adult male and prepubescent boy. Even so, the relationship was not considered a homosexual affair in their society.

That's one possibility. Remember, though, the word *arsenokoites* was not used as a word except by Paul initially. It shows up four hundred years later, being translated by the early Church father, Jerome. Interestingly enough, in 383 A.D., Jerome translates the word as a *male prostitute.*

When Jerome lived, the Roman Empire was still intact. Much of the society that Jerome was looking at was similar to the society that Paul was looking at. Jerome, in retranslating the word *arsenokoites* would think it referred to something obvious to him. Male prostitution as part of pagan religious rituals also was very common in the early Roman Empire. Male prostitution in Paul's day was often associated with pagan religious rites within the pagan shrines. It was a prevalent part of pagan worship rites in Roman temples. In the city of Rome alone, there were 420 temples for different gods and goddesses. Each deity had its own temple. Within those temples, worship activity incorporated temple prostitution.

Therefore, when Jerome in 383 A.D. translated *lift couch*, to him it seemed obvious to be a male temple prostitute. That is another possibility. However, equating male prostitution with homosexuality per se is in much discord and inaccurate as equating all female heterosexuality with female prostitution.

Though *arsenokoites* could have been a temple prostitute, the word *malakos, soft,* could have been something else, totally unrelated, that was very real in Paul's day. The word soft can also legitimately be translated as *jelly-like* or *spineless*.

What was happening in the Roman Empire in Paul's day? Christians were being persecuted. Paul himself helped in the persecution in the former days of his life. More than once great persecution arose against the church.

These were times of trouble. Saul made havoc on the church. Christians were hauled to prison. Christians were crucified, beaten, and thrown to lions and gladiators for public sport. Herod the king had James; the brother of John killed with the sword. He proceeded to arrest Peter as well. [Acts 12:1-5].

Persecution continued long into Paul's ministry. He mentioned how many ways he was in danger. He was in danger from false brethren or spies in the church. He had been beaten with thirty-nine lashes several times. Several times he was stoned. He was left for dead. This volatile atmosphere caused even Apostle Peter to back down from the truth, not only at Calvary but also in Antioch, for fear of persecution. [Gal. 2:11-20]. Barnabas also was carried away with Peter for fear of public opinion. Many became opponents of the truth from within the ranks of the Church. Diotrephes, (mentioned in the Epistle of 3 John), Hymenaeus, and Alexander, who Paul said made a shipwreck of their faith, are a few of the many who are mentioned.[22]

Several of these converts fell away and became traitors. Persecution breaking out caused people to behave in weak-willed ways. When a Roman soldier had his sword at your throat demanding to know whether you were a Christian, lots of believers lied and said no. Some people were soft. Some people were spineless. Some people were *jelly-like*, because with a sword at their throat they too ran away from Christ and denied Him as in the garden of Gethsemane.

In the meantime, others were asked if they were Christians, with a sword at their throat, and they said yes. They faced the gladiators. They faced the lions. They were burned alive. They were crucified. They were thrown in jail. They lost their homes, their lives, and all worldly possessions. There were many martyrs, as in Smyrna and Pergamos [Rev. 2:8-17].

Some of those spineless ones came under the conviction of the Holy Spirit. They repented. They realized they could not afford to deny Christ. They repented and came back to the Church. But they came back to those who had now lost their martyred loved ones for their confession of faith, while these others had denied Christ. This was a very real issue faced by the early church. Should they forgive these deniers of Christ and bring them back into full fellowship or deny them access to the secret meetings of the church? The early Church at first did not trust Paul after he had seen Jesus. How much more were these others distrusted? Yet if *malakos, soft,* meant spineless, Paul could have been saying to the Corinthians, but such were some of you. But now you are changed. They could easily look around the meeting room and nod, yes that's so.

In all these instances, whether it was the man who sexually exploited his slave boys, or seduced the freeborn youths, the idolatrous male priest-prostitute, the young male hustler, as Mark Anthony was said to be, or the spineless as *malakos,* they were changed. And in any of these cases, they would no longer be who they once were.

SANCTIFIED GAYS

Reading again from I Corinthians 6:9-11[23],

1 Cor 6:9-11

9 Do you not know that the wicked will not inherit the kingdom of God? Do not be deceived: Neither the sexually immoral nor idolaters nor adulterers nor [*malakos*], nor [*arsenokoites*] nor thieves

196

nor the greedy nor drunkards nor slanderers nor swindlers will inherit the kingdom of God.

11 And that is what some of you were. But you were washed, you were sanctified, you were justified in the name of the Lord Jesus Christ and by the Spirit of our God.

Whoever Paul is talking about as *malakos* and *arsenokoites* will not inherit the Kingdom of God, if they stayed in their former state. If the words malakos and arsenokoites were talking about homosexuals, as many churches and traditions insist, then what would a washed, sanctified, and justified homosexual be? Would a washed, sanctified, justified homosexual be a *heterosexual?* If that were so, as some traditionalists try to assume, then every gay person who ever becomes a Christian would automatically be heterosexual. We know that every idolater, every temple prostitute, and every thief who ever came to Christ in a real sense, was changed and no longer lived as they once did. If these words meant homosexual, then you would have to say that every homosexual who came to Christ became a heterosexual. But we know this is just not so. A washed, sanctified, justified homosexual is a homosexual who has been washed, just like anybody else who has come to Christ, but a homosexual, nonetheless.

Ask the parallel question: what a heterosexual is who is washed and sanctified and justified? Do they stop being sexual after they get saved? No. But the way they live out their heterosexuality changes. They became more responsible.

They don't find the need to go into single bars every night to make a new sexual conquest, or cheat on their spouses and commit adultery. Although these things do occur even among Christian heterosexuals, if they are living for Christ, they come under conviction and know they're not acting properly in a way that now honors God. They still function heterosexually, but differently, because they're washed.

The same would apply to gays and lesbians.

As was reported in the May 1990 edition of *Keeping in Touch,* the publication newsletter of the Universal Fellowship of Metropolitan Community Churches,

"Michael Bussey and Gary Cooper, the founders of Exodus International, a Church based coalition of "ex-gay" ministries have denounced all such programs seeking to convert homosexuals into heterosexuals, according to articles in *The Sentinel* (2/2/90) and *the Bay Area Reporter* (2/8/90).

Bussey remarked of the programs "I had no success with them. I counseled...hundreds of people... who tried to change their sexual orientation, and none of them were successful. If you got them away from the Christian limelight and asked them "Honestly now, are you saying that you are no longer homosexual, and you are now heterosexually oriented?' ...not one person said "Yes, I am actually now heterosexual."'.

Bussey became a family counselor for gay and lesbian couples. He admits that his past work did "psychological damage...There may very well be people out there that I talked to who are dead because they committed suicide because of the guilt I inadvertently heaped on them. I feel guilty about that. I mean it was well-intentioned. I was getting brainwashed by the church; this is what I was supposed to be doing. But it damaged me; it damaged the people I talked to.

One man, according to the pair, suffered such psychological damage that he mutilated his own genitals with a razor blade in a desperate attempt to rid himself of his sexual desires. Another impulsively underwent an incomplete sex-change operation because he believed his sexual desires might receive Divine approval if he were biologically a woman.

But at the time "I was convinced it was working." Bussey said. "Every once in a while, a crack in that conviction would occur. I'd ask, 'How come I'm still having these feelings?' I'd see a Christian psychologist, and he'd say" Oh, that's just temptation. Ignore it or suppress it. You are different. You are now ex-gay. You're no longer gay. Those feelings don't mean anything."' But the feelings didn't go away for either of the men. In fact, even during their tenure with Exodus, some "Ex-gay" counselors actively engaged in gay sex, even after a full day of "ex-gay" counseling.

Both said they experienced such inner conflict that they decided to leave the organization in 1979. They altered a talk they were scheduled to give before the general synod of the United Church of Christ, to the shock of the audience they called for the acceptance of gays and lesbians as they are. That stand spelled a rapid end to their involvement as speakers of organized evangelical Christianity. Soon after, they moved in together.[24]

When people try to define *arsenokoites* as unqualified homosexuality, they see it doesn't work. But whatever Paul was referring to does work. It couldn't have been homosexuality, per se, otherwise, homosexuals would *all* be ex-gays once they became Christians. That would be it. They wouldn't have to worry about it anymore. It doesn't happen that way. A lot of gay people try to fool themselves, but one day they wake up and realize they are still gay, though Christian, as Mr. Bussey points out.

[1] 2 Corinthians 13:1

[2] 1 Cor 15:29

[3] *Strong's Exhaustive Concordance of the Bible.*, see dictionary section of New Testament Greek Words.

[4] ibid.

[5] *Strong's Exhaustive Concordance of the Bible.*, see dictionary section of New Testament Greek Words.

[6] ibid.

[7] *New Englishman's Greek Concordance and Lexicon*, Wigram-Green, Hendrickson Publishers, Peabody MA. 1982

[8] Strong's Exhaustive Concordance of the Bible., see dictionary section of New Testament Greek Words.

[9] pg. 89 *What The Bible Really Says About Homsexuality* by Daniel Heminiak, 1994, Alamo Square Press, San Francisco, CA.

[10] [#3120] malakos

[11] Spirit-Filled Life Bible, New King James Version, Jack W. Hayford, General Editor; Thomas Nelson INC., Publishers; Nashville, U.S.A.; 1991, pg. 1726

[12] Ezekiel 16:49-50

[13] Boswell, John (1980) *Christianity, Social Tolerance and Homosexuality: Gay People in Western Europe from the Beginning of the Christian Era to the Fourteenth Century.* Chicago: University of Chicago Press.

[14] Scroggs, Robin (1983) *The New Testament and Homosexuality: Contextual Background for Contemporary Debate.* Philadelphia: Fortress Press

[15] Lambert, Royston, *Beloved and God: The Story of Hadrian and Antinous,* Zebra Press, Alexandria, VA, October 10, 1996

[16] Scroggs., pg. 36

[17] Scroggs, pg. 38

[18] Plutarch, *Erōtikos</i> 768F*

[19] Scroggs, pg.39

[20] ibid., pg. 40

[21] Scroggs, pg.41 / Cicero, *Philippics* II 44f. / Josephus, *Antiquities* XV. 23-30.

[22] 1 Tim 1:19-20

[23] *The Holy Bible: New International Version,* electronic ed. (Grand Rapids: Zondervan, 1996, c1984), 1 Co 6:9-11).

[24] "Ex-Gay Ministry Founders Recant" *Keeping In Touch,* Universal Fellowship of Metropolitan Community Churches Newsletter, May, 1990.

Epilogue

I wish I could tell all the stories of what God has been doing in the last 50-plus years. But I don't know them all. I feel more like Frank Bartleman [1] who was best remembered for his chronicles of the 312 Azusa St. revival in Los Angeles which lasted from 1906-1909. He was an eyewitness and a historian who wrote of the things he saw. There are so many other women and men God used in this movement and God is not finished by any means. I wanted to lay the foundation for people to see how this happened in the beginning. And I pray those whose names I forgot to mention will forgive me, and even better yet add their own stories to this expanding history.

Since the beginning of this movement, many branches and streams have started.

Author Justin Lee began a conference where gays and straights come together to have civil conversations. He is an American author, speaker, and LGBT Christian activist known for his focus on building bridges between groups who disagree. He is the author of *Torn: Rescuing the Gospel from the Gays-vs.-Christians Debate*, and the director of a 2009 documentary, *Through My Eyes*, which explores the struggles of young gay Christians. He is also known for founding the Gay Christian Network [2], which he ran from 2001 to 2017. Currently, he is the executive director of Nuance Ministries.[3]

Another young author who is responsible for a large following and who holds conferences to discuss reconciling homosexuality and Christianity is Matthew Vines.[4] His book, *God and the Gay Christian: The*

Biblical Case in Support of Same-Sex Relationships [5] started a serious conversation among non-gay and LGBT Christians on reconciliation.

[1] frankbartleman.blogspot.com last accessed August 2, 2022

[2] https://en.wikipedia.org/wiki/Q_Christian_Fellowship last accessed -1-6-2020

[3] https://en.wikipedia.org/wiki/Justin_Lee_(activist) last accessed 1-6-2020

[4] http://www.matthewvines.com/ last accessed 1-6-2020

[5] https://www.amazon.com/s?k=matthew+vines&i=stripbooks&crid= 29OD54VYS2UHY&sprefix=mathew+vines%2Caps%2C175&ref =nb_sb_ss_sc_2_12 (last accessed 2-29-2020)

The Covenant Network

B ut after the Advance conference more or less blew up, the churches in that fellowship were left without any organized plan for Christian fellowship. Our friends Evelyn and Dennis Schave kept telling us "You have to meet Pastor Randy Morgan in Atlanta!" I kept hearing this time and again. I wondered what that was all about. It turns out that Rev. Randy Morgan pastors an LGBT-affirming church in Atlanta that is fully engaged in the moving of the Holy Spirit.

The Immersed Conference of The Covenant Network in Atlanta.

On July 23, 2000, Bishop Randy Morgan saw ten people gather together at the pool house in the apartment complex in which his husband, Pastor Johnny Layton, and he lived. They assembled for the first meeting of the New Covenant Church of Atlanta. This began a new move that soon extended beyond a local church in Atlanta.

Just as we did, Bishop Randy Morgan invited evangelists Evelyn and Dennis Schave to preach revivals at his church. Then one year he and I were both invited to be guest speakers at SpiritFest. The next year, he was again a guest speaker, and Jerry and I attended. By now I was starting to see what Evelyn and Dennis were trying to tell me. We were on the same page in hearing from God. Rev. Randy Morgan's church, New Covenant Church of Atlanta began hosting a conference called Immersed.[1] From this conference began a network of Spirit-filled affirming churches called the Covenant Network. This annual conference in July has hosted about 500 LGBT-affirming Christians. This slowed down when COVID made large gatherings stop. For two years the meetings were online only. In 2022 they began once again in person and online. In-person registrations were limited to 200 people. I was blessed to be there with my husband, Jerry. It is a dynamic flow of the Spirit. Once we began going, we only missed one, because Jerry and I were moving from Ohio to Florida at the time. Currently, this is the largest gathering of LGBT affirming Christians who come together in one accord to worship and serve the Lord Jesus. The presence of God is undeniable.

This is one incredible weekend in the presence of God.

Matthew Shepherd

Matthew Shepherd changed the playing field

Matthew Wayne Shepard (December 1, 1976 – October 12, 1998) was a gay American student at the University of Wyoming. On the night of October 6, 1998, he was alone at the Fireside Lounge and befriended by two roofers, men who pretended to be gay to lure him to go with them. The pair saw an easy target in the 5ft 2in, slightly built student. Aaron McKinney and Russell Henderson drove Matthew to a desolate plain near Laramie, Wyoming, and Henderson used a clothesline to tie Shepard to a log fence. Then they brutally beat him, pistol whipped him, tortured, and left him to die in the cold. Eighteen hours later, while in a coma, he was discovered by a cyclist.

When first discovered, his rescuer thought he must be a scarecrow; he was so badly beaten he didn't look human. He was taken by rescuers to Poudre Valley Hospital in Fort Collins, Colorado, where he died six days later from severe head injuries.[2]

Matthew was an Episcopalian. He went to church. God used his martyrdom, in that his death, which revealed the physical danger that homosexuals still faced, resulted in the 2009 passage of legislation that expanded federal hate crime law to include the sexual orientation of the victim.[3]

Even though much of the world recognized Matthew Shepherd as a martyr, and that his death changed the playing field for gays in America; the Rev. Fred Phelps of the Westboro Baptist Church in Topeka, KS, arrived to picket the funeral. His signs proclaimed "God Hates Fags" which is the name of his website [4]. For many months afterward the website had a picture of Mathew Shepherd surrounded by flames with a male voice screaming. An automatic clock below the picture counted how many days "Matthew had been tormented in Hell". Now that Fred Phelps is dead, the website has moved on to other targets to attack. I would give presentations to college classes on Homosexuality and religion and would always pull up the "God Hates Fags" website to show that religious discrimination was still strong.

[1] https://www.theimmersedconference.com/ last accessed 1-6-2020

[2] https://en.wikipedia.org/wiki/Matthew_Shepard **(last accessed 2-29-2020)**

[3] https://www.britannica.com/biography/Matthew-Shepard (last accessed 2-29-2020)

[4] http://godhatesfags.com/ last accessed August 2, 2022

Morals, Jezebel, (AIDS) and Marriage equality — and God

At the beginning of this movement, back when Rev. Troy Perry first got the vision to start a church where gay people would be welcome, gays were not welcome in society, much less in church. As a result, meeting other gays was often a secretive affair. People were afraid of being caught. Once arrested, police would call employers and newspapers would print the names of gays who were arrested. Your job, livelihood, and reputation could all be ruined in one day. Many cities had their police departments entrap gay men and arrest them. The American Psychiatric Association and American Psychological Association considered homosexuality a sickness that needed to be cured up until 1973 at the earliest. And the religious right, the Moral Majority (Jerry Falwell, James Dobson, et.al) used language that fostered fear and hatred against gays. Transgender people were barely even on their radar back then. As a result, though some couples would form, and live a secretive life, it was more common for gay folks to have furtive one-night stands or secretive liaisons. Bathhouses were one avenue for these encounters. So were public parks with wooded paths or underground gay bars whose Mafia owners paid off the police. I personally saw this happens. This lifestyle flourished until the advent of AIDS.

In the book of Revelation, (Chapter 2:18-28) the church in Thyatira has a woman named Jezebel whom God judges. She causes God's people to commit sexual immorality. The woman so named is led by a demonic spirit named Jezebel. This would be the same evil spirit that led Queen

Jezebel of ancient Israel to be an apostate and lead God's people away from Him to serve Baal. Both women were judged and have long since died. But the spirit that led them, remained on the Earth, still seeking whoever it could seduce into sin. Ephesians 6:12 says *for we do not wrestle against flesh and blood, but against principalities, against powers, against the rulers of the darkness of this age, against spiritual hosts of wickedness in the heavenly places.* Jezebel is one of those principalities. It had the gay community by the throat and dragged us around like puppets.

Sexual outlets and liaisons flourished and were exploited through fear (of being caught and exposed/ arrested) and proliferated by lust. But as the Holy Spirit began to move in the midst of the gay community, lust and hopelessness were replaced with love and commitment. Little by little, the LGBT community started to see we had a right to live, work, and love. This shift took place simultaneously with the rise of Christianity and the Holy Spirit's move among the gay community. No longer did one-night stands seem acceptable, because something better was being provided — love and commitment to a lifelong partner. MCC recognized this shift, and before it was legal, began providing Holy Unions, commitment ceremonies for couples, celebrated by and within their affirming church family.

Then it became apparent, that Holy Union or not, the government would not recognize our relationships and still treated couples as if they were legal strangers. So, when one partner would die, the remaining partner had no more rights than a roommate. Families who had rejected and abandoned their gay child would suddenly swoop in like a vulture and strip the remaining spouse of everything; house, car, bank account, furnishings, everything, and all legally sanctioned. If a will had been made, it would be challenged in court. Yet the Holy Spirit kept moving in the legal arena as well. Suddenly and amazingly — even miraculously, on June 26, 2015, the Supreme Court of the United States ruled that marriage equality for all couples was a constitutional right. The religious right and their churches vehemently fought this. Gays did not have the resources, or even the legal standing to make this happen. We were still considered as if we were "sick criminals". But God kept changing public opinion, moving us forward in the media, the legal system, the courts, and His church. And God used people to make this happen. During this whole season, marriage became the expectation among LGBT Christians and the norm. Morals were raised to a higher level, and God became the center of LGBT Christian homes. No such thing was ever possible before God stepped in.

The Ideological War Rages

B ack in the 1990s I met weekly with other local pastors in Dayton, Ohio to share their lectionaries and to see what scriptures they'd be considering for the next week's sermon. We had many times of prayer and conversation. Even then the local Dayton Methodist minister said the acceptance of homosexuality would be the next Civil War within the church world. And just as she predicted, it is happening within the Methodist church.

What was the problem — why were we not accepted as full partners in the gospel?

So many ministers are just stuck in their understanding of what scripture means that they cannot see what God is actually doing. Franklin Graham, Billy Graham's son was reported to say, in his understanding of Scripture, that gays should be killed.

In an article by Bil Browning

Thursday, July 12, 2018, it was reported that *Franklin Graham tells Jimmy Carter that Jesus would kill gay people, not marry them*

He stated: that Jesus wouldn't bless gay couples, Instead, God would kill them all. Jesus didn't come to promote sin, He came to save us from sin," Graham wrote. "The Bible is very clear. God destroyed the cities of Sodom and Gomorrah because of homosexuality. God defines sin in His Word--it's not up to our opinion, the latest poll, or a popular vote."[1]

Yet, despite this dogmatic stance by many in the Christian community, there are many prophetic voices who are starting to hear the voice of God tell them that He is bringing in wounded outcasts into His family. Many, many prophets had such things revealed to them over the last twenty years. However, as they speak this, they really have no idea of whom God is speaking. A gay friend of mine, Len Van den Berg, also a prophetic voice within the LGBT community responded to an article found in *The Elijah List [2]* back on 2/24/2004 by Jon Hamill of Lamplighter Ministries.

In the article, Hamill shared that after he had seen gay couples on the steps of the courthouse of Boston MA, he felt the need for America to pray. Subsequently, he had a dream and felt a need to pray for America. Especially since gays were moving forward in their demands to be recognized. He felt this was very, very wrong. He wrote:

This brings me to my third prophetic experience, which was simply a whisper from the Lord while praying over the gay marriage issue that has brought Boston, Massachusetts to the forefront of the news lately. The Lord spoke that "Inconvenient Intimacy" is set by Him to overthrow "Illegitimate Intimacy."

It has been amazing to see the massive gatherings of gays and lesbians at the Statehouse on Beacon Hill in the city covenanted to the Lord as "A city on a hill, a light to the nations." They are gathering to convince politicians that their expression of intimacy should be legitimatized by a law allowing them to marry. As Massachusetts is a major root of our nation, what transpires in this pivotal state often finds expression across the land — "For if the root is holy, so are the branches."

It is therefore interesting to note the proclamation this state carries on its license plates — "Massachusetts, the spirit of America." What spirit will prevail in this region covenanted to God by our forefathers? What is God asking us to do on behalf of the land in this season of inconvenient intimacy? Bigotry and hatred only mar the countenance of Christ as expressed through His people. Truthfully, we have no option but to pray!

Please pray for Boston, and for the Northeast. Pray for leaders and intercessors in the region and nation to be strengthened by the Spirit. Pray for gays and lesbians to find and please be sensitive to the whisper of the Holy Spirit that is now a mandate for our land. Whatever the cost, it is time to gather together for fasting, repentance, worship, and intercession in this season of inconvenient intimacy. Please let us heed God's invitation to gather for a "Second Call"--- the experts are needed at this time!"

Len answered this prophet as follows:

February 25, 2004

Dear Jon,

It was with great interest that I read your writings in the Elijah List this morning.

I also took note of your writings on illegitimate Intimacy.

I grew up in a Pentecostal Home. I was called to ministry at a very young age, being baptized in the Holy Spirit, etc., etc. from 10 years old. I left our Pentecostal Church when I was 19 and became part of a strong Charismatic Megachurch in South Africa. Here I received sound and solid training and teaching in the Word of God. I played the piano and was called to be a Worship Leader for many years in a few churches in SA. I married a precious wonderful wife at age 25, and we were together for a good 10 yrs.

However, I knew from a young age that I was gay. I spent many nights in prayer asking, believing, and praying for deliverance. I was prayed for, and every conceivable demon was cast out, etc., but I stayed the same. One day the Holy Spirit started speaking to me and I realized my angle was wrong.

God pointed me to a scripture in Matt 19:12 and said: "Len, do you know I made you this way?"

I was astounded, as I was always taught it was evil and wrong to be gay and it was demonic.

God said to me I was gay because He made me this way, and for a good reason. I needed to come to a place in my walk with God where I accepted this, and He would begin to use me.

At a number of occasions, people visiting our church would call me out and prophecy over me that God called me to be a prophet. I was 23 at the time, and although had a partial prophetic anointing on my life as a result of the Praise and Worship ministry, I realized it was not my time yet.

When I was 35, my wife and I were divorced for good reasons. I could not hold her away from a life that she would find fulfilling any longer, and we remain very close even today. She has remarried. Last year in November God started dealing with me very strongly again. I was kicked out from the church where I was when I revealed that I was gay, and I found a home, like many others like me, in the MCC Charismatic wing.

I had a prophetic dream recently where God spoke to me and sent me to be a voice of healing and direction to hurting people God wanted to pour His Spirit out upon. I experienced that the Holy Spirit pointed some truths out to me that were twisted over the years by those in Charismatic circles and God showed me how these people used God's word to clobber and hurt God's people. Just as they did by condoning slavery in the previous century; God wanted to reach those gay people that the rest of the world so easily and readily want to stone. But He would have to raise up those within the LGBT community to do so since they would see the potential harvest field there that nobody else dare to go into.

And so I responded to God's call. I have a wonderful Spirit-filled partner, and we are experiencing that God is moving mountains in our church and community.

The Holy Spirit revealed to me that He is already speaking to some prophets about hurting people. God will bring healing and restoration to them too. The word EUNUCHS in the Old Testament (Is 54) is a widely used term to include anyone not being able to have a heterosexual relationship.

I discovered that God DID NOT destroy Sodom and Gomorrah because of homosexuality, but rather for reasons given in Ezekiel 16:49. Here God is clear as to the reasons why He destroyed Sodom and Gomorrah. Jesus also healed a gay man. Look at the servant of the Roman Centurion. The Greek word here is *pais*. This means "lover boy", not servant, and Jesus knew it. He understood the context of the culture of that time.

I also found that The Leviticus laws against acts of homosexual sex had to be understood in context. Go back to the original Hebrew and Greek to find answers. God did not want Israel to follow the Canaanites' practices. They would often have sex with the temple priests as a sacrifice to Moloch. God hated idolatry with a passion.

God then told me He had a promise for the Gay and Lesbian community. If we

hold fast to His covenant and follow Him, He would give us a name better than sons and daughters. (Is 54).

We are holding fast to that promise. God has not forgotten us, and I believe that we are a vital part of the body of Christ He is going to restore. The key to this restoration will be Praise and Worship. It will bring unity to the Body of Christ in a new dimension. The Word says, "One of us will put a thousand to flight, but two of us...." Can you imagine the power the Church will have when a united Body of Christ starts waging war against the forces of darkness, for this reason, the enemy is doing all he can to prevent this unity from coming about. His strategy is to sow hatred and mistrust in the straight element of the church, thus keeping the Church divided.

God also told me we need to get new wineskins as He is going to do this restoration and those with old wineskins, mindsets and theologies, will not be able to contain this.

Sir, could it be possible that God is doing something in the Gay Community to prepare them for Harvest?

On this side of the fence, we are praying and doing warfare so that God will tear down the walls that divide and separate. I believe God is challenging you today to change your wineskin, peek over the fence and come and see what God is doing inside the MCC and Gay Community.

The MCC in Long Beach LA CA is a prime example of a Church reaching out

and preparing its people for harvest. God is moving there. We know it and feel it. I live in London UK, and we hear the same trumpets blowing. And it thrills and excites us to know we are hearing the trumpets.

Some prophets are also speaking about this people God is raising, a hurting and rejected people, but to this day they are not sure who God is talking about...

We are right under their noses... I trust you will allow God to reach deep inside you to show you what He is doing.

To him who has an ear, let him hear what the Spirit is saying.

Len

From the desk of Len Van den Berg

[1]   https://www.lgbtqnation.com/2018/07/franklin-graham-tells-jimmy-carter-jesus-kill-gay-people-not-marry/ Last Accessed 1-18-2020

[2]   elijahlist@qwest.net, https://www.elijahlist.com 2/24/2004

https://www.elijahlist.com/words/search_results.html?keyword=&author=&day=24&month=2&year=2004&submit=Submit

Conclusion

Though there are a few other scriptures that could be considered, it is beyond the scope of this book to review them all. Refer instead to my other book *Openly Gay, Openly Christian, How the Bible Really Is Gay Friendly*. Instead, I wanted to give a few New Testament examples of how the Holy Spirit has brought about a fresh understanding of Scripture to the new move of God that He has been doing within the LGBT community.

We needed answers for the abuse LGBT people have suffered at the hands of the Christian community. We were only told we were dirty, perverts and criminals. As God began to move, how could we reconcile the outpouring of grace with the things we'd been told? It was the work of the Holy Spirit who gave us insight and revelation as to the intent of scripture regarding the LGBT community. Suffice it to say, God showed up in our midst, beginning in 1968, and has continued pouring out His Spirit on all flesh.

Colossians 1:12 says God made us qualified to be a partaker of the inheritance with the Saints. God alone qualified us to inherit the Kingdom of God. We couldn't do it. We couldn't make ourselves fit. We can't save ourselves; God did this. We were once in the clutches of death and God came along, without the Church's permission, and set us free! God delivered us all from Satan's power. Then God transferred us into the Kingdom of His dear Son. Not because we deserved it. Not as a reward for anything. But God did it through the Blood of the Son of God, and because of His love for us.

The church called us reprobates and degenerates. They refused to eat with us or share communion with us. They refused to come to our bedside as we were dying of AIDS. But Jesus came. By His love, we are changed and transformed. And despite the political sound bites of the religious right, we still grow from glory to glory. Our orientation remains the same, but we live our lives now transformed and snatched out of the oppression of Satan into the liberty of the Son of God. We are known by a new name, written in the Lamb's book of life. We are the Whosoevers (John 3:16) and the redeemed of the Lord.

We are washed by the Blood of Calvary. Praise God, He did it all, and it is freely given to whoever will receive it! And now and then, to their great surprise, other Christians who want to get closer to the heart of God get a peek at His beloved gay children.

One scripture God has used to bring insight and revelation to the heterosexual allies among us was found in Acts chapter 10. In this passage, Peter, a good Jewish believer, and one who followed the Jewish laws was given a vision of non-kosher animals on a lowered sheet and told to rise, kill and eat. He refused, objecting because it was against God's law. God then said what He had cleansed, not to call unclean. But soon Peter discovered that God was not talking about food, but people. God had cleansed gentiles, starting with Cornelius, a Roman soldier. God keeps doing that. For people who would be called unclean by the Church, God cleans them up and presents them to the Body as bona fide brothers and sisters in Christ.

Yes, the Holy Spirit began moving in our midst in 1968 and hasn't stopped. He showed up in a hospital room and began calling home His little lost lambs who had been thrown out to the wolves by the flock. He picked us up, he rescued us, He pulled thorns out of our wool. He made us lie down in green pastures. He led us beside still waters. He restored our soul. He prepared a banqueting table for us in the presence of our enemies. He anointed our head with oil. He whispered into our heart that He loves us and that He is and forever will be our Good Shepherd. He will never leave us. He will keep us in the palm of His hand, ever pressed against His heart.

Jesus loves me this I know. For the Bible tells me so.
In John 10:16 Jesus says:

16 And other sheep I have which are not of this fold; them also I must bring, and they will hear My voice; and there will be one flock *and* one shepherd.

He never says who these OTHERS will be, but throughout history He keeps surprising the church with whom He brings in.

God isn't done yet, either. There are still others that Jesus has in mind. And they are also welcome as children of God. Whosoever believes in Him should not perish but have everlasting life. There are still lots of Whosoevers out there. And to those, I say Welcome Home!